POSTCARDS FROM WITHIN

Postcards from Within

Random Ramblings of an Ordinary Human

a memoir by Savita Harjani

BEAVER'S
POND
PRESS

POSTCARDS FROM WITHIN © 2023 by Savita Harjani

Beaver's Pond Press is committed to turning interesting people into independent authors. In that spirit, we are proud to offer this book to our readers; the story, the experiences, and the words are the author's alone.

Cover and interior illustrations by Arushi Mittal
Book design and typesetting by jamesmonroedesign.com

ISBN 13: 978-1-64343-616-6
Library of Congress Catalog Number: 2023901693
Printed in the United States of America
First Edition: 2023
27 26 25 24 23   5 4 3 2 1

Beaver's Pond Press
939 West Seventh Street
Saint Paul, MN 55102
BEAVER'S
POND
PRESS
(952) 829-8818
www.BeaversPondPress.com

To order, visit www.savitaharjani.com.

Contact the author at www.savitaharjani.com for speaking engagements, book club discussions, and interviews.

To my friend, Ramesh Harjani.
Without you,
this journey would neither have been possible
nor amazing.

Watching you suffer, I thought, was the toughest thing I have done. Letting you go, turns out, is tougher. You were grace and elegance personified until the very end. I am grateful that your suffering has ended, but how do I fill the huge void in my heart and soul? Until we meet again, Ma. I hope you and I will always be mother and daughter in every lifetime. Be at peace, my *pukka dosht*.[1]

May 11, 2020

CONTENTS

FOREWORD

V erbosity does not necessarily convey depth and substance that any speaker or author wishes to convey. There is no substitute for simplicity of expression. "Brevity is the soul of wit," said Shakespeare's Hamlet.

In the leaves of this book, the reader will find a very beautiful collection of Savita's thoughts. Written over the years and inspired by moments of intense experiences, Savita has penned her feelings, thoughts, lessons drawn, and generally, her spiritual growth in life. In the powerful yet simple words penned by Savita, one can relate intimately with an overt echo of one's own personal and intense experiences. Different in time and space, different in race and culture, different in the personal extent of experience, yet very much a reflection of life that may well be identified as our own.

What particularly marks Savita's work is her ability to express a world of meaning with minimal use of words. She inspires her readers to conjure up a mental image of the experience she shares with her simplicity of expression. Indeed, the brevity of her words mask the enormity of her thoughts and experiences. The mind of the reader is able to unpack the beauty of the experiences in its own way, relate to them in their personal life, and enjoy the wisdom and learning in the same way as conveyed by the author.

I have found myself spiritually richer. I have found solace for many of my own struggles. And I have found a reference upon which I may rely to help me define many of the confusing feelings I may have. I have enjoyed every word. I have no doubt the reader will too.

—Arvind Gupta
Senior Legal Officer, UNHCR
Pretoria, South Africa

INTRODUCTION

Dear Reader,
If you are reading this, you have bestowed upon me the most precious gift of all, your time, for which I am enormously grateful. My purpose in writing this letter to you is to give you an insight into what prompted me to indulge in these musings and, further, what has prompted me to share them with you. These were originally written with an audience of one in mind—me.

Most of the thoughts that I share in this book arose during the time period from 2016 to 2021. I am a lawyer by profession but moved to India to become the primary caregiver for my mother, Kanta Gupta, who was suffering from chronic kidney disease (CKD). She was concurrently diagnosed with esophageal cancer. Suffice it to say this was an exceedingly challenging period in both our lives. Coming face-to-face with and exploring my own vulnerabilities and failings constitutes a large part of the *postcards I have received from within*. My thoughts over this time period have meandered all over the place without any common-sense organization to them, from God and faith to social media and politics, but have primarily been an observation of my own shortcomings. These musings were recorded because, many times, writing them down was the only outlet I had.

I moved to the United States as a twenty-year-old. And all my life, I knew that the day would come when the pillars of my life would start to crumble and need my support. My biggest fear was that when that time did come, I would have to choose between my life in America and my responsibilities toward my mother in India. My husband and I would often on a Friday evening, a glass of wine in hand, talk about what we would do when the time did come. And in 2016, it came. It was time to put our money where our mouths were. But the Universe was so kind and generous that the way it played out was not as a difficult choice but rather as an empowering joint decision that my husband and I made together to experience the privilege of taking care of my mother in India. I say this without arrogance but with some amount of satisfaction that when the time did come, we did not hide behind reasonableness and rationality. The move to India for a period of five years was not an easy one, and by most standards, neither was it reasonable. My husband's role in supporting me physically, emotionally, and financially in this endeavor was even more unreasonable and irrational and worthy of my undying gratitude and awe.

Life has given me the opportunity to experience it in its rawest form, up close and personal. And I am sure it has many more surprises in store for me yet. There are certain human emotions I have experienced and aspects of life I have observed on my journey thus far that I will share with you. As I am not unique in having been exposed to life, a description of my experiences and observations is something that I have in common with my fellow humans. *Cliché* is a term defined almost universally as anything that has become trite or commonplace through overuse. But when I add my layer of personal experience to something that is commonplace and trite, it becomes cliché no more. It has the legitimacy and credibility of my having experienced it firsthand. I express these personal experiences in my own way, unique to what I have experienced, but they are similar to what others have gone through before me and will go through after me. I believe this is called the human condition.

Now I come to the reason I have chosen to share these musings with you. Over the years I took care of my mother, every once in a while, I would share some of my written thoughts with her. I was with her constantly, and every time something struck me, I jotted it down in my phone. Ma saw me intensely engaged with my phone, and she figured out what I was doing. On occasion, she would ask me to share with her what I had written. My mother was an incredibly intelligent and thoughtful woman. She would hear me out, contemplate what I had said, and then engage me in some philosophical discussions. She dealt with not one but two diseases, each a giant in its own right, with dignity and courage. She never lost heart. However, 2020, the last year of her life, was exceedingly difficult. She started to become increasingly withdrawn. I can only imagine the kind of pain she must have been in because she never complained. Around May 7, 2020, it became apparent that it was now a matter of time. She became very quiet. Not only did she not want to talk, but she was also unable to talk. On May 10, she beckoned to me, and when I came close to her, she put her hand over my head and said, "*Tu likh*"— you write. These were her last words to me; these were her last words on earth. On the night of the eleventh, I held her hand as she silently extinguished. One moment she was there, and the next, she was not.

I recorded my thoughts as an outlet for what I was going through. Most of the time, I was unable to share my thoughts with others because those who loved me would have been pained by my struggles. And even if I were to have shared, no one was in a position to alter or lighten my situation. Further, life was teaching, and I was learning. I did not want to lose the insights

I was gaining. Lastly, I just wanted to write. This memoir originated with no intended audience, so I was able to jot down my feelings uninhibited. I hope the fear of being judged and embarrassed has not deterred me from sharing myself with integrity and authenticity. I share these musings with you for the sake of sharing them. I also know that loss and grief are not unique to me. Perhaps you will identify with some of my struggles, or perhaps it will just give you a different perspective on life.

I stand before you, through my words, vulnerable and humbled. For I am not a writer, and I do not excel in the art and craft of communication through efficient use of language. But my thoughts are simply stated and authentic. They truly are the postcards I have received from within.

—Savita Harjani

POSTCARDS FROM WITHIN

THE EARLY YEARS
OF CAREGIVING

*I feel nothing but gratitude for the privilege bestowed upon me
to be able to take care of the one who gave me life
and took care of me.*

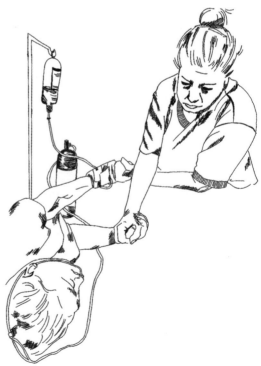

Role Reversal

*Watching a parent fade is the
opposite of watching a child grow.
Ma fades and extinguishes a little every day,
she is my baby now.*

*Ma experienced a labor of joy
when she brought me into this world,
I experienced a labor of sadness,
as I helped her exit this world.*

*When I was little, Ma exclaimed,
"Oh look, she can stand on her own now."
When Ma was eighty-five, I exclaimed,
"Oh! Ma can't stand on her own anymore."*

*Ma said about me, "She ate her first solid food
today, she is growing up so fast."
I said about Ma, "She can't eat solid foods anymore,
let's try liquids, maybe she will be able to swallow."*

*Ma was so excited, "My baby is responding,
she is starting to understand language."
I was so sad, I think Ma is starting to
lose comprehension, she is staring at me blankly.*

*Ma called my father and gushed,
"Our baby has said her first word."
I called my brother and said,
"Our mother has forgotten her first word."*

*Ma exclaimed, "Yay, poopies on
her own for the first time."
I asked, "Ma, is it time to have*

a conversation about diapers?"

*Ma exclaimed with joy, "It is so
exciting to watch her grow every day."
I whispered with pain, "It is so
sad to watch her extinguish a little every day."*

*Ma said thoughtfully, "Before you know it,
she will be all grown up and will leave me."
I said with grief and finality, "Before you
know it, she will have extinguished and left me."*

A child develops by leaps and bounds. Before their first birthday, a child changes from being stationary to running all over the place and acquiring a million skills and learning a million things. I saw the opposite happen with Ma. Within months, she went from independence to dependence. Within months, she forgot things that took her a lifetime to learn and remember. Within months, I went from being her daughter to becoming her mother.

I thought this period of my life was a devia-
tion my life path had taken. But it turned
out that for the duration, the alleged detour
was my life path. My life path was what I was
on, not what I wished it to be.

Dear Life,

I want you to know that I love my ma intensely. I feel nothing but gratitude for the privilege you have bestowed upon me in giving me this opportunity to care for her. My thoughts that sound like complaints are simply my physical and emotional limitations arising from my humanity. Not for one second would I trade a moment of the mother-daughter time you have so generously given me. I implore you to not misunderstand my rants stemming from my own limitations and vulnerabilities.

Gratefully yours,
The Ordinary Human

I am grateful to life for giving me the opportunity to experience it a little bit more in the raw. And I am under no illusion that the tough times I am going through are probably mild in comparison to how tough tough times can get. In my tough times, my love and support have remained uncompromised. Money is sufficient to meet all my needs and even indulge in some indulgences. Why am I complaining? I should have no emotion other than gratitude. I am sorry. I am grateful for the life I have, and I would not trade it for anyone else's. I am grateful for the lessons I am being taught, and I am grateful that the curriculum is not tougher than it is.

In the early days when dialysis was a new part of our daily routine, it took some getting used to for everyone involved, particularly Ma. Coming to terms with her new normal was not easy, but Ma was a fighter. She processed the fact that life had changed permanently and that there was nothing that could be done to go back to life before dialysis. She resolved to accept her new life with an amazing attitude and spirit. Once we would release her from her overnight tethering to her dialysis machine, she would be ready to embrace the day with a fighting spirit. She would charge into the dining room ready for her breakfast. Her dialysis belt was a permanent accompaniment to any outfit she wore. It housed her dialysis catheter and was black in color, sort of like a martial arts black belt. She named herself the "dialysis ninja." Such was her spirit until the very end.

Ma was on sixteen hours daily peritoneal dialysis. We did the procedure at home. We used to connect her to her dialysis machine overnight. We would detach her from the machine in the mornings, and the machine would leave the last round of dialysis fluid in her, which we would drain manually each afternoon. This afternoon time with Ma was very special. It took nearly an hour to drain her. She and I would listen to music and share stories, and it became a wonderful bonding time for us. Ma and I talked about everything under the sun, from politics, philosophy, God, religion, family, and relationships to our very intimate, private, and personal thoughts and experiences. For the first three years that I took care of Ma, before things got really rough, this was my favorite time of the day. We shared so much, and I learned so much—about life, about her, and about me.

Once during one of our precious dialysis afternoons, Ma shared something wonderful with me. She said that every once in a while, she experienced a feeling, a sensation of joy or satisfaction or happiness, near her diaphragm. She said she tried to pinpoint it and hold on to it to experience it for longer, but the sensation was fleeting. She also said that she got various smells, such as the smell of earth. Not just petrichor, but the smell of the earth even without rain. One smell she described was that of *aag ki tapan*—the smell of the heat emanating from fire. She asked me if I knew the smell, and I did not. She said it was not the smell of the smoke or the wood or the coal or the object in the fire or the fire itself. It was the smell of *tapan*—the smell of heat itself. What a beautiful share; it made me incredibly happy. It made me think that the two smells she described were two of the fundamental elements of life—fire and earth. How interesting. I wondered if this had a deeper significance. I was blown away that someone going through such a rough time in life had the capacity to perceive such positive, energetic thoughts. I was inspired and so proud to call this woman my mother.

One day Ma and I were discussing the concept of time. I said to her that the way we can tell that time has passed is by seeing the changes in things, concepts, emotions, and people—everything that time touches. We look older; we know time has passed. The hands of a watch have changed position; we know time has passed. We are no longer having a good time, or the quality of time we are experiencing has changed; we know time has passed. Day turns into night; we know time has passed. Bald trees bear delicate, fresh green leaves that turn to lush dark green, changing to reds and yellows before shedding altogether, followed by a snowy white cover; we can tell time has passed. But what if we were to live in a vacuum with nothing to observe that would indicate change? Would time pass? Does that mean change is time? We do not know time; we only know change. When I had this thought, it felt like a revelation of a universal truth. I am sure if I researched the issue, I would discover that science has much to say about it. But for now, I am content with the question. Is change time?

On another occasion, during our precious afternoon dialysis bonding hour, Ma shared an interesting story with me. Ma was three when she lost her mother. She said that when I was an infant who had just learned to sit up, I used to gaze at her very intensely, follow her with my eyes as she went about the room, and then sigh deeply. She said it was quite an odd behavior for a child so small. My father had also witnessed this and had remarked on a couple of occasions, "I think this child may have been your mother in her previous life." Possible. Regardless of the possibility of such an occurrence, it was a story that I cherished. I did not have my own children, and now I was caring for my mother as though she were my own child. I love her so much. And if there is any such thing as reincarnation, I wish she and I would alternate being mother and daughter for eternity until salvation.

Ma was a very thoughtful and intelligent woman. She would share little bits of her thoughts with me, which often ended up to be serious words of wisdom. I cherish her words and often draw upon them for guidance in life. One day, during one of our afternoon dialysis sessions, Ma was in a pensive mood, and I was not sure what she was thinking about. She then said, "Beauty is not safe. It attracts people that destroy it." She further added about beauty, "It makes the beautiful arrogant and unable to protect itself. It is also short-lived." Ma was a wise woman.

You know you are really close to someone once you have tweezed their facial hair. My ma and I both have been blessed with facial hair. It has taken me a lifetime to make light of this situation and see the humor in it. One time, my brother was coming from Botswana to visit Ma. During our afternoon session, I said to Ma, "Ma, if we do not groom ourselves, when Bhai[2] arrives, he will wonder what happened. He will have come to see his mother and sister, and instead he will find a father and brother." It was amazing to see Ma so genuinely amused, and we both had a very hearty giggle. It was a precious moment, and as those were so few and far between, I can still recall it with clarity.

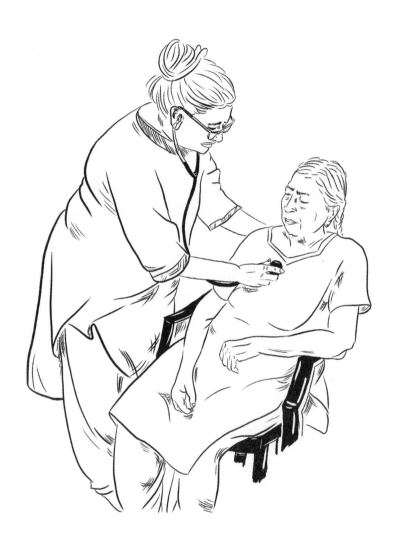

As Ma's primary caregiver, I had become a half-doctor. I had learned enough about nephrology to be dangerous. I had learned enough to converse intelligently with Ma's doctors—sufficient to annoy them. I had learned enough that the hospital staff would ask me if I, too, was a doctor. My sister-in-law, who is a doctor, taught me how to use the stethoscope and the manual blood pressure machine. Ma had always wanted me to become a doctor. One day when I was using a stethoscope on her to report back to the doctor if her chest sounded clear, I saw Ma shaking her head. When I asked why, she simply said, "I told you, you should have become a doctor!" I did like taking care of Ma. I found I had even become a decent diagnostician. It was like being a detective, putting the puzzle pieces together to get a better picture. In hindsight, I think I would have liked being a doctor. Alas, it is too late for this lifetime. I will add it to my list of "should haves."

Our routine in Delhi was that with our morning tea, Ma liked to listen to *bhajans*—religious songs. Some were wonderful because they narrated interesting stories, while others were enjoyable because the music was excellent, or the singer had a beautiful voice, or the beat simply got you. Some, on the other hand, filled me with rage for multiple reasons. These bhajans were the sort that instilled fear in people, making them God-fearing instead of God-loving. They spiritually and emotionally blackmailed people. And then there was the hypocrisy. One bhajan in particular compelled me to write this thought. In Hindu mythology, Lord Krishna is often portrayed with dark skin coloring. The bhajan narrated a story wherein the devotee singing had his heart stolen because he was so taken by the dark skin of Lord Krishna, completely losing himself in a state of joy and bliss. The accompanying video had all these people dancing, and very poorly at that, to the lyrics. I would wager my life on this—not one of these devotees would accept a dark-skinned daughter-in-law for their sons unless they had no choice or were so greedy that a large dowry would make them momentarily overlook the color of the girl's skin. But only momentarily. Once the dowry was in, the poor girl would be taunted until her dying day for the color of her skin. We Indians, we are not racist as such, but we do an excellent job at discriminating based on skin tone. I shared this thought with Ma, and that was the last day that bhajan was played in our house in Delhi.

Even though we had settled into a daily routine, I longed for normalcy in my life. When I would say, "I want my life back," it did not mean I was praying for things to end in India. I did not know how to make Ma better and independent and at the same time have my life back. I would often say to myself, "Are the two even possible together anymore? If not, then this is the life I choose. I do not wish for my old life back. My present is what it is, and my future will be what it will be. All I need now is courage, strength, patience, conviction, and a generous dose of all virtues that will get me through."

During this phase of my life, the single greatest thing life was trying to teach me was to stay in the moment. The instant I stepped even one toe out of the moment, everything fell apart. One day I wrote, "Today I wish this were not my life. I feel like I am being punished. Is my misery coming from how challenging it is to be a 24/7 caregiver? Or is it coming from what others are doing and what I am missing? I think the latter, because caring for Ma is a privilege. And in caring for her, I am always in action, which is very fulfilling. But the moment I get distracted from my goal, the misery commences. I have to remain in the moment. I cannot envy others' joys and successes nor derive solace from their failures. I have to remain focused on what I am committed to doing. Sometimes, like today, it may not be a pleasure to play the caregiver. But I know it will always be a privilege, and for that I am grateful." Life had created such circumstances for me that I was unable to wish for two of my most heartfelt desires at the same time—to be with my husband and for my ma to have as long and healthy a life as possible. For the fulfillment of one was a certain unfulfillment of the other. So I wished for neither. I did what I needed to do. The insight life gave me was that I could only live the moment in the moment. I had memorized this lesson. But the wisdom of the lesson had yet to materialize.

I thought a lot about the power of the almighty "moment." Life always changes in a moment. It is in an instant that life reveals some fact, or some decision is made, or something happens, that alters the course of one's life forever. A few examples illustrate this point. As one checks the results of a career-defining exam, that moment of eyes on the result alters the course of one's life forever. As one proposes to their beloved, the moment of a positive or negative response alters the course of one's life forever. As one holds a lottery ticket and compares the winning numbers, the moment of matching winning numbers forever alters the course of a life. As a doctor diagnoses a dreaded disease and declares a shortened lifespan, the moment of declaration changes everything forever. The events leading to the revelation of the moment may be a long time in the making; however, the knowledge rendered by the moment is what alters the course of a life. And even the almighty "moment," the moment it gets spent by virtue of having revealed its secret becomes a benign unit of time in the past and is archived for its historical significance as a life-altering moment. I grasped the importance of the Moment on the day when I walked into the doctor's office and waited for him to tell me whether or not Ma's cancer was back. The revelation of that moment could have made it the worst moment of my life, but in this instance, the Moment gifted me relief. It could easily have gone either way. How would I have broken the news to Ma, how would I have managed, how would I have endured watching her suffering become more intense. But on this occasion, I got to be the bearer of good news. All in a moment's work!

I found the epiphany about the power of a moment to be very intriguing. I started to think about it a lot. One day I thought that my insight into the power of the moment sounded very much like the concept of Schrödinger's cat, a thought experiment by physicist Erwin Schrödinger[3]. Without going into details, my layperson understanding of this experiment is that until you look in the box, the cat is both simultaneously dead and alive, its fate being linked to a random subatomic event that may or may not occur. The concept made me think that looking in the box is quite akin to my epiphany of the power of the moment. Until the truth or the fact is revealed in the moment, life could go either way. It is the moment of knowledge that has the power of making the cat either dead or alive. I am not a physicist by any means, but my almighty "moment" sure sounds like life or death for Schrödinger's cat—Ma both had cancer and did not have cancer until her report was read to me by her doctor.

I never thought that my musings would venture into the realm of physics. First came Schrödinger, and then the principle of the observer effect.[4] Another concept from physics, this principle states that "observing a situation or phenomenon necessarily changes it." The reason I thought of this principle is you! The moment I decided to expand the audience beyond me to include you, things changed. I would extend this a step further and say that even the anticipation of observation changes the situation or phenomenon to be observed. For the case at hand, the moment I anticipated your eyes on this work, this body of work started to get modified by a process called editing. And when your eyes actually rest on this work, it will be further modified by the fact of your having viewed it. You may perhaps interpret ideas in your own unique way, and you may assess this body of work favorably or not. Regardless, your interaction with these words will alter my words forever.

Because Ma was a dialysis patient, we, her care team at home, needed to keep everything clean and sterilized. We used to wash our hands over a hundred times a day before touching her for any reason. One summer, our water supply in India got contaminated with sewage water. The city itself declared the water unfit for human consumption and usage. We were buying bottled water to meet our water needs, an entirely unsustainable solution. More than two weeks elapsed, and the city had taken zero steps to fix the problem. It was not a problem for anyone else in the neighborhood because everyone had their own water wells, which was impermissible by law. My parents being extreme rule followers, ours was the only house in the neighborhood without one. Given the city's inaction, I was forced to get our own water supply. I was left with no option but to create my own water supply, and I was confident my actions were justified as self-defense. Our society allows self-defense as a justification to excuse the taking of a human life by another when it is in the protection of self or another. This was only an administrative rule, but without this action, my mother's life was in serious peril.

The whole water situation got me thinking about Gandhi, on his birthday, coincidentally.[5] If memory from high school history serves me well, Gandhi was once arrested for intentionally violating a law. The judge did not want to penalize Gandhi for said violation. However, Gandhi insisted on being punished and informed the judge that he had no choice but to dole out punishment or resign for not upholding the law as it stood.[6] My predicament with this water situation was similar but on a miniscule scale, and I am no Gandhi. In addition to not having Gandhi's courage, commitment, and brilliance, my then-current responsibilities were of a very personal nature, leaving me no bandwidth to stand up for causing social change. And frankly, nor did I have the desire to do so. So, my expression of self-righteous indignation at this water situation had to suffice to absolve me of the responsibility of actually doing something about it.

I love righteous indignation. It appears to be a great mechanism by which one can absolve oneself of all responsibility of having to actually do something about the thing that causes the indignation. By expressing anger or displeasure, one distances oneself from the undesirable thing and ensures that everyone knows they are not like the people or situation causing the indignation. And it somehow also seems sufficient in terms of having done something to denounce the situation without actually having to strain oneself to cause worthwhile change.

While I was taking care of Ma, Ma was taking care of her older sister, my *masi*. *Masi* means mother's sister. My masi had taken care of all her siblings all her life and had never married herself. Ma had lost her mother in the most tragic of circumstances when she was three years old and was cared for by her older siblings, particularly this aunt. When Masi became quite ill, Ma felt it was now her turn to take care of her sister, despite the fact that she herself needed a caregiver. Masi had been ill and bedridden for several years. One morning, it started to become apparent that Masi was now with us but for a brief time. On the morning of November 13, 2016, around ten o'clock in the morning, we knew the time had come. Masi's eyes rolled back in their sockets, she stopped blinking, and her breathing became labored. I sat with her, stroking her hair and calling out to her, reassuring her that it was okay, and she could let go. While sitting with her, awaiting the end of her life, I thought of reincarnation. If there is any truth to this theory, this incredibly sad and painful experience must have a corresponding incredibly happy and joyously anticipated event. My masi was in labor of death, and I was helping her through it, and somewhere in the world at that very moment, there must have been a woman in labor, happily anticipating the birth of her child. At births, we are all so happy and never stop to think that somewhere in this world, there is a family in mourning and missing a family member. If there is any validity to the idea of reincarnation, the labor of birth and love must have a corresponding labor of death and grief. They're two sides to the same coin.

Dear Life,

Death has a smell, and unfortunately, I know it.

Yours,
The Ordinary Human

My masi and I always had a bit of an edgy relationship. She loved me tremendously and I her. Our solitary issue centered around the treatment of my mother's longtime domestic help. In India, we use the reprehensible term *nauker*, which means "servant." In our home, that word was never used, nor were people treated with disrespect; this was the law laid down by my parents. Masi, on occasion, would take exception to the fact that we would not side with her when it came to the domestic helper. I should actually just use his name, because he is a key character in this story and more than a brother to me. His name is Omi. Omi was well protected from the wrath of Masi. But this would always cause friction between her and every other member of the family. (This is a long setup for the point of this thought.) My masi would have given her life for anyone related to her by blood. She did more than reasonably possible for her siblings, nieces, and nephews. She treated us like her children and made sacrifices so we could have things that our hearts desired. When Masi passed away, all my thoughts turned to how much she had done for us. All the negative thoughts fell away. Why is it that when people are alive, they can do no right, and once they are dead, they did no wrong? This question led me to this powerful life tool: I think eulogizing the living would be a good mechanism to be able to let go of petty issues and annoyances and focus on why people are important in one's life.

Dear Masi,

I think of you a lot. I miss you, and I wish I had been kinder. I wish I had thought of eulogizing you while you were still with me. You have my love and gratitude for all you did for all of us, in perpetuity. I know you had a very hard and lonely life. I am sorry I was not more understanding. I hope you are at peace wherever you are and have joy in your heart.

Love you to eternity,
Your niece

Dear Life,

I think I am going to write eulogies for my living loved ones. Eulogies are for the living and not for the departed. Eulogies should not be words filled with regret to assuage our feelings of guilt but rather tools to help us put to rest our petty differences and grievances, to say things we never say, and to find a way to move forward. Eulogies are always for the living, and my dearest ones, I want you to be validated, acknowledged, and celebrated while you are alive and for you to know how important you are to me.

Humbly yours,
The Ordinary Human

Dear Omi,

To the world, you are a servant, an abhorrent term. To me, you have earned your place in the same class of extraordinary men as my father and husband. There is nothing reasonable or ordinary about you. Your station in life is nothing more than a happenstance of birth. I am filled with gratitude for your role in my life.

Gratefully yours,
Didi, your older sister

Dear Omi,

Aapne zindagi ki subah se zindagi ki sham kardi, sewa mein. Iske liye hum sadaiv aapke aabhari rahengi. Ya to aapne koi wrin chukaya hai, ya hum aapke wrini rahenge—*"You have spent from the dawn of your life to the dusk of your life in service. For this, we will forever remain indebted to you. Either you have repaid a debt, or we are now in your debt."* Thank you, dearest brother Omi. We may have been born to different mothers, but there is no doubt that you are Kanta's son and my brother.

With love, admiration, and gratitude,
Your didi

One day Ma and I were resting in the afternoon when Omi came and gave us some terrible news. *Didi,*[7] my older cousin sister, had suddenly and unexpectedly passed away. This came as a complete shock. Didi lived in the neighborhood, was a doctor, had her own hospital, and had helped care for my aunt. She was barely sixty and fairly healthy. She was a good soul and cared about people. I went to her cremation and observed an interesting phenomenon. It was such a tragic event and solemn occasion, yet we humans conducted ourselves with decorum but for a very brief period of time. Once the pyre was lit, slowly but seamlessly, the conversation at the cremation ground shifted back to the living. We went from condoling to socializing and catching up. The departed became a sideshow. What does this say about us? We all know that this is going to be our ultimate end, whether cremation or burial, yet we somehow must believe that this end will escape us. Else our behavior at such places is inexplicable. It was a fantastic and humbling observation.

At Didi's cremation, I experienced some new emotions, and I recorded them. I wrote, "I am at the *shamshan ghat*—the cremation ground. Didi's body is being prepared for the last rites. She is being surrounded by wood. In traditional families, only men can do this job. I am watching. There is a neighboring body that is ablaze. Once all the rites are completed and the body is well on its way to being reduced to its elements, custom requires that it be left alone. That body's family has left. It is now by itself and engulfed in a roaring fire. The wind has changed direction, and there are ashes from that pyre flying and falling on all of us. Parts of it are on me. I do not know any of the criteria on which to prejudge the individual that the body would have been. I do not know gender, age, marital status, sexual orientation, religion, caste, class, social stature, nationality, level of education, profession, looks, or anything else about the departed soul upon which I could have formed an instant opinion as to whether or not I was going to like this individual. I just have bits of it on me, and I feel a sense of freedom and connectedness to the universe in a very bizarre sense that may even be considered uplifting. It is all so bizarre. It should be horrifying to be surrounded by burning bodies, yet it is oddly peaceful. What a strange place! What an amazing place! It equalizes all."

Dear Life,

I have been thinking about my experience at the cremation grounds. As hard as I tried, I couldn't distinguish myself from the burning body. I was one with it because I was not separate from it. That feeling of connectedness and oneness is a powerful and uplifting emotion. I am so grateful to you for showing me that we are all one and we create artificial distinctions to separate ourselves from each other. Thank you for this insight!

Humbly yours,
The Ordinary Human

To perform the last rites for someone, to restore their body to the elements, is a privilege. To be in a position to give another human being the last bit of dignity as they depart this earth so their body does not languish and decompose, that is indeed a privilege. In the Hindu context, this is not an easy privilege to hold. Giving of last rites is a very raw and humbling act. I have had this privilege on three separate occasions and feel blessed.

My husband is my hero for taking the road less traveled, for doing the right thing with quiet, dignified anonymity. Ma is my hero for being grace, elegance, and generosity in the face of so much pain and disease. Papa is my hero for having the power of mind over matter, for being the veritable optimist. Omi, my mother's attendant, is my hero for showing me what unwavering commitment and loyalty look like. My brother is my hero for showing me how to accept life as it comes. The character of Patrick Jane from the show *The Mentalist* is my hero for showing me what not needing external validation looks like. Life right now is giving me challenges to overcome so I can become my own hero.

I have been told I am wonderful and brave for looking after my mother. I feel neither wonderful nor brave. I feel grateful, overwhelmed, sad, and like a failure. Grateful because it is truly a privilege to have the opportunity and resources to care for my mother. Grateful because I am married to the most amazing human being and help is coming from places I would never have imagined. Overwhelmed because I do not know how and for how long I will be able to manage all there is to handle. Sad because I do not know how to help Ma. She is struggling so much—I can neither make her happy nor well. Like a failure because I feel like the slowest kid in class who is unable to grasp this simple lesson: that life is temporary, death is inevitable, and pain and suffering are our constant companions. Neither can I grasp nor accept these fundamentals of life.

The job of a caregiver is without breaks. I have not stepped outside the house for about three weeks. I have no professional or social interaction. Some people have called me stupid for abandoning everything and being in India. Some have called me a hero for abandoning everything and being in India. I am neither. Why am I doing this? I am doing this because I love my mother. I am doing this because it is the right thing to do. Is there such a thing as the right thing to do? I do not know. What makes it the right thing to do for me? Not doing the thing that I believe to be right will make me so guilt ridden that I will not be able to live with myself. The absence of guilt and presence of love makes it the right thing for me to do. But I am so tired. Yes, I am so tired. I am discovering that managing guilt and the presence of love are insufficient reasons to do what I am doing. I am learning that what separates a commitment from a "should do" is choice. I am committed, and short of a physical inability to perform by reasons of death or disease, I am going to do this. Fatigue, exhaustion, irritation, isolation, loneliness, stress, depression, I see you. But you shall not deter me from my mission because I chose to do this. I do this not because it is the right thing to do but because I chose to do it. An epiphany—I am finally starting to get the distinction of "choice." It is pretty powerful. Without choice one cannot accomplish anything, because the reason for doing things will always change or become redundant, or the cost of carrying on will become overly burdensome. At some point, one will give up unless one is doing something out of choice. I choose; therefore, I do.

My current reputation is that of being a good daughter. In society, my previous alleged misdeeds seem to have been forgotten for the moment. Right now, I am a good daughter. But my humanity with all its failings will inevitably come through. I am realizing that being placed on a pedestal is a tough place to be. It feels great while the tenure lasts, but the fall from grace is long, hard, and tough. And fall one must. It is important to remind the world of one's humanity and all its failings, particularly while still perched on the pedestal, so the inevitable resulting disappointment does not come as a complete surprise.

I have to do what I have to do. What others say doesn't matter. Their words of praise should not elate me, and their words of criticism should not dismay me. Words are just words. How I react is what gives them power. Today I read somewhere that "true power and strength is in not reacting." Observing and then doing what needs to be done is the solution. Action, not reaction. Every time I instinctively want to react, I should think for a second before opening my mouth. Restraint is powerful. I will get there. Or rather, I am trying—I may get there.

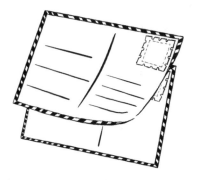

The desire to be good is compelling in most people. Everyone likes to be thought of as a good person. Being good is not always easy. Every once in a while, I succeed at being good and then feel good about it. One day I died and reached the Land of Gods. To borrow from Harry Potter and J. K. Rowling, upon arrival, I was ready to be sorted into my future place of existence. At the high table were seated Buddha, Shiva, and Jesus. Playing McGonagall's part was Lord Krishna. He placed the sorting hat on my head. There are three houses in the Karma School of Humans and Humanity—Heaven, Hell, and Earth. As soon as the hat was placed on my head, it said, "Difficult, very difficult. I see a lot of good. But where to place you?" "Not Hell, not Hell," I kept muttering. "Not Hell, you say? You will have fun there; a lot of your friends are there. But if you are sure, better go back to Earth, because even though there was good, you were aware of the good. There was some arrogance and holier-than-thou attitude. You felt superior about being good. Earth it is. Maybe next time, you will just do good for the sake of it and not be superior about it or judge others. You are not there yet." Back to Earth I came. Waaaaaah, waaaaaah, a new baby is born. And so that's how reincarnation works! And for me the journey commenced anew. Maybe I will do better this time.

Being exposed to mortality in ways that I had not been before made me wonder about God. I do not know whether there is God or not. But I am beginning to understand humanity's need to have God. When one is going through a rough patch in life, as I am right now, and has no control over the circumstances, it can be reassuring to think that there is a higher power that is ultimately responsible and will come to one's rescue. Or should one drown and not be rescued, the existence of a higher power, at least in the Hindu context, gives one a level of bizarre comfort that it is the result of some karmic accounting over several lifetimes that one was deserving of such unwanted fate. While going through this current challenging patch in my life, somewhere I allowed myself the comfort of the possibility of God. This in itself was not a problem. The problem came when I allowed fear and superstition to become part of the equation. While standing with folded hands in Ma's temple, I would watch closely the facial expressions of this one particular picture of God Rama. Some days it appeared to be smiling, and some days it appeared to be stern. I started to take the smiling face to mean the day would go well, but the stern face predicted a rough day. Back to the beginning of this thought, I do not know if there is God, but regardless of the truth, I cannot allow myself to be consumed by fear and superstition. I have plenty on my plate already. If there is God, I hope he[8] will help me. If there is God and he does not help me, there is nothing I can do. And if it turns out there is no God, I am on my own anyway.

Dwelling more on God, fear, and superstition—in the construct of our society, universally it seems that God, fear, and superstition are a package just like software updates. When updating one's computer, many of us non-techies and even many techies do not realize that there are essential updates and optional ones. All updates are checked for download by default. Unless one takes the effort and is confident about the update choices, one will end up with the entire package. Similarly, in the God context, an overwhelming majority of us do not realize that to believe in God, one doesn't have to download the programming related to fear and superstition. But it takes a great deal of courage, faith in self, conviction in one's beliefs, and logic to withstand the pressures of society and so-called God Men from participating in rituals and behaviors based on fear and superstition. I wonder if it is possible to separate God from fear and superstition. I wonder if it is possible for me to separate God from fear and superstition.

Dear Life,

When you do not make any sense and when I have no control,

God becomes the default explanation.
Destiny becomes the default responsible party.
Karma becomes the default justification.
Hope becomes the default prayer.

Today I am relying on God, destiny, karma, and hope. Maybe I will make it, maybe I won't.

Bewildered, but yours,
The Ordinary Human

A further analysis on God, fear, and superstition: If there is a God, I hope he is a benevolent God. In which case if I do what I need to, then I expect him to do what he needs to. If there is a God and he requires worship and praise rather than having his creation do the right thing, or requires worship and praise in addition to us doing the right thing, I am not sure I can swear allegiance to such an entity. On the other hand, if there is no God, I am on my own anyway. I hope it is either the first or the last. Preferably the first.

Dear Life,

*If God told me right now, "Ask and ye shall receive,"
I would not know what to ask. Am I that content
or that clueless? Or maybe deep down I know that
nothing that can be asked for and given can hold the
solution to salvation.*

*Yours,
The Ordinary Human, yet again*

I say I do not believe. Yet I keep begging someone to give me strength and bestow faith upon me. If I do not believe, who am I asking? Why this desperate desire to connect with something beyond me? The desire to believe is strong, yet there is something that does not allow me to let go of my skepticism. I want to believe because life is tough, and I do not want the buck to stop here with me.

I want to believe in God; I want to have faith. Faith can give a lot of strength. But one cannot fake faith. I cannot fake faith. I want to draw strength from my beliefs and not have them weaken me. If having faith means becoming not responsible for myself, I shall have to struggle through life in my current state of incompletion and confusion.

One day I told Ma that I did not believe in God. Ma was a person of unshakeable faith. She was neither disappointed nor angry at my sharing. She was amazing. She did not try to convince me that I should have faith. She simply asked me if I believed in her. I said, "Yes, of course." She then said, "If you believe in me then you must believe in my father." I said, "Yes." She then informed me my grandfather was God. She was the real lawyer in the family—not my dad, not my brother, and definitely not me.

If there is a God, why does he allow people to abuse him? He is bribed in temples, churches, and other places of worship, falsely advertised, and even slandered. From what I have heard, he is supposed to be omnipresent, omnipotent, and omniscient. Why doesn't he do something about it?

I really would like to believe in God. At some level, I probably do. I just cannot align with the prevailing popular model, regardless of the religion. It is so jarring. Churches and mosques are easier to relate to as architectural monuments. But I have baggage with Indian temples—I cannot see them as places where God resides nor as architectural touristy monuments.

I believe in karmic accounting. It is a fundamental belief I hold in life. If this assumption is invalid, I will be lost, and I will not be able to deal with the unfairness and injustices of life. If there is no karmic accounting and evil can succeed without consequences, I just cannot make any sense of life. But I do not think I am wrong about this. Further, if there is any validity to reincarnation, it explains karmic accounting across lifetimes. If one cannot make sense of an unfairness or injustice in this lifetime, one can console oneself by saying that this is carried over from a previous life. Even if the assumptions of reincarnation or a higher power doling out justice are fallacies, one's own conscience and guilt are one's own reward and punishment. Even if one faces no societal consequences for a wrongdoing or succeeds at deceiving everyone and convincing the world of falsities, I believe that deep down, one cannot escape oneself. The guilt has to be its own punishment. Similarly, on the positive side, the satisfaction of doing the right thing has to be its own reward. If it is not so, nothing in life makes sense.

Jane		Good Ka	Doe Bad Karma	Ending Balance
Lifetime	Starting Balance			
1	0.0	+31.4	−96.57	−65.13
2	−65.13	+106.5	−36.78	4.59
3	~~	+36.52	−10.58	~~
4	30.53	+68.2	~~	82.46
~~	82.46	+~~	~~	~~
~~	~~.55	+~~	−~~	~~
50	~~	~~	~~	~~
~~	~~			

I do believe in karmic accounting. But I wonder how God keeps track of it all. For a moment, I will shift my position from that of an agnostic to a person of faith and assume that there is a God, and he keeps an accurate account of karmic activity—the good, the bad, and the ugly. How does he manage these accounts so precisely? There are approximately eight billion of us down here on Earth. Well, if we humans can create a whole banking infrastructure to manage money for a gazillion accounts with enormous amounts of money, God could surely have come up with a better system to manage karmas. I imagine that our souls come with an inbuilt accounting mechanism, and all transactions, good or bad, get entered into the karmic ledger in real time as they occur. I also imagine that, unlike manual or software glitches that can impact bank accounts, karmic accounts are error proof.

For me, the biggest curse and the biggest blessing is the same— "May your karma be with you." It is a safe curse. If I curse someone unfairly because of a misunderstanding, then the curse will actually work as a blessing, and I save my own karmic account from being depleted because I wrongly cursed someone.

I have been thinking about reincarnation a lot lately. Ma has been extremely sick, and I do not know how long I have her for. Will she be reborn? Will we meet? I perceive her as an evolved soul. It feels to me that the innate wisdom and contentment she carries within her must have been collected over an immeasurable period of time. In observing her and those less wise and less at peace than her, it appears to me that what a soul needs and what it can give are inversely proportionate, depending on its maturity. A younger soul needs more and can give less, whereas a mature soul needs less and can give more.

Like there is muscle memory, I hope there is soul memory. I am inclined to think there is. I would hate to lose the lessons I am learning so painfully this time around and repeat the same mistakes in the next lifetime, should there be such a thing. People appear to be at various levels of a soul's evolution—soul memory makes sense.

When I was little, one day I said to my mother, "I hope you come as my daughter." I did not realize the significance of this. To have Ma as my daughter, I would have to lose her as my mother. Coincidentally, the way life worked out, I did not have children, and I did not get to be a mother. But Ma gave me the opportunity of experiencing motherhood. In her last days, I took care of her as my child. I experienced being a mother to her. My grief was double upon losing her, for I grieved the loss of my mother and the loss of my child. If there is a next lifetime, I hope we will be mother and daughter again.

A corporation has shareholders. The boss of the company is the CEO. The CEO reports to the board of directors and is subordinate to it. The board, in turn, reports to the shareholders of the corporation. Many shareholders are also employees. So, the CEO, who is the ultimate boss of the shareholder employees, in effect is answerable to said employees. It completes a full cycle. Applying a similar analysis, is God ultimately subordinate to his devotees?

The trust Ma bestowed upon me led to a massive sense of responsibility. My decisions regarding her health were critical. A wrong decision could have ended her life sooner. The enormity of this responsibility paralyzed me. But the urgency of the moment and the necessity of a decision compelled me to act, right or wrong. I developed a mechanism to mobilize myself from a paralytic state. I would say out loud the reasons for making a particular decision and to the best of my ability, made sure I took everything that I could into account. Then I would place myself in the future where typically one would be faced with the consequences of a decision. Standing in that future, I would assume that the decision I made was the wrong one. I would then return to the present moment of decision-making, and, given everything I knew in that moment, if I would make the same decision again, I would act. If at a future point the decision turned out not to be the best, I would process it as the correct decision with unintended consequences. And I would forgive my future self in the present decision-making moment for deciding on a particular course of action that my future could potentially encounter as wrong.

While taking care of Ma, it occurred to me that not being able to watch a loved one suffer and be in pain is more about self than the person suffering. It is painful for *me* to watch Ma in pain. *I* cannot do anything to make her feel better. Realization dawned that it is always about me. I had to come up with a strategy to be effective in the face of this failing. To be there for Ma, I had to be able to shift the focus away from me and my pain arising out of my helplessness of watching her in pain so that I could function and be effective.

Another incident that convinced me that it is always about us and not the other person, no matter the situation, was when my husband expressed a desire to take flying lessons. I was not at all excited at this prospect. I tried for a while to get him to change his mind. I argued that this was a dangerous activity. It was for his own good that I was preventing him from pursuing his dream. I added that there are many small planes that crash. I informed him that he may be injured or even die. He was being foolish in wanting to embark on this adventure. One day I was minding my own business, and this insight hit me unexpectedly. Of course, a disclaimer is in order at this point: I may have left the practice of law, but the practice of law did not leave me. I am not advocating this position in the case of children or others with diminished capacity, but I digress. It occurred to me that when I was trying to stop my husband, the love of my life, from doing something he really wanted to do because it was risky or dangerous, I believe in so doing I was expressing my love for myself more than my love for him. Because I could not bear the thought of living without him, I was willing to sacrifice his happiness for my own sake. I think the honest reason that we dole out tough love is that we do not want to lose our loved ones, watch them suffer, or have to take care of them because of their foolishness. Tough love is not unconditional. It comes with conditions. It is selfishness disguised as selflessness. I am happy to relay that, post-insight, my husband has completed his solo flight and is well on his way to test my unconditional love for him every time he leaves solid ground.

Dear Life,

Today I am tired, and my thoughts have wandered into the realm of extreme disempowerment. From this state of disempowerment, another facet of responsibility that has revealed itself to me is that responsibility is when you want to end it all but will not because someone depends on you for their survival.

Responsibly yours,
The Same Ordinary Human

Dear Life,

Today the enormity of the responsibility of being a caregiver has hit me hard. Ma trusts me implicitly. She eats and does what I tell her. Any medical questions that arise, she looks to me for answers. She has placed her life in my hands 100 percent. Please help me. Let me do the best I can. Oh, let me not make any mistakes. Let me make the right decisions. Please let me live up to that trust that has been bestowed upon me. Let me be worthy, and let me not let my mother down.

Overwhelmed but yours,
The Ordinary Human

I do not think there is any right or wrong thing to do. Nor is there a judgment in taking responsibility or not taking responsibility. To test myself, I ask if I am feeling guilty or bad or if I feel I ought to have done something that I did not. These are private tests. No one sees me take them, nor does anyone ever find out whether I passed or not. However, I myself can hardly escape the outcome of these tests. There seems to be no choice in taking the test either, even if I do not want to take it. The test gets taken, and the result gets declared—all in the silence of my mind.

Dear Life,

Today I really don't like who I am being. Am I really that not nice? I don't have one pleasant thought. So much anger at the world at large for my failures. Do you think anyone can tell? Do you think this shall pass?

I think it has passed. When it occurred to me that perhaps I was not as nice as I thought I was, it was a humbling moment. Then pretty much in the very next moment, it occurred to me that because I realize I am not as nice as I think, it makes me nice and more enlightened than some who may not have had this realization yet.

Just the Ordinary Human,
Rolling her eyes again

When I take the easy way out and do not do what I know I need to do, I am filled with guilt, excuses, and justifications. Not taking the easy way out makes my excuses and justifications fall off. There is a certain inner satisfaction that compensates for the fatigue I experience by taking the harder path I know to be right. My success is not in succeeding; it is in doing my best as authorized by my heart.

How did I get to be the person where the buck stops? I did not ask for this. Today, in this moment, I feel like such a failure, so lost, so alone, so sad, and so incredibly angry. I better snap out of it fast because these feelings will not make the buck stop somewhere else. If I do not take responsibility, things will downward spiral, and in an instant all my efforts will become garbage. It is so bloody annoying that it takes a damn lifetime to build and earn credibility but only a moment to destroy everything.

I had an insight into feelings—rather, how I feel at a given moment in time. Sometimes life is hard, and the moment feels oppressive. Some other moments fill me with joy, and I feel light-hearted. I have discovered that an oppressive moment is actually a good moment because things can only get better once I have hit rock bottom. By the same token, a top-notch joyous moment is a risky moment because it is bound to change, and as it is already the best, it can only be less than what it is now. The instructive part of this insight for me is to just stay with it—neither the bad nor the good will last. It all averages out. When in the dumps, find joy in the expectation of good things to come. When on a high, enjoy it while it lasts, for it will change soon enough.

I am the acting head of Ma's household. I am learning that the mood of the household aligns with the mood of the head of household. I now have the added responsibility of managing my moods. I cannot give in to the temptation of sulking or allowing myself to feel low. It is not easy being a leader.

The buck stopping at me gave me an insight into leadership. Leadership does not necessarily have to be a grand affair. One does not need to be the CEO of a large company or a politician up to changing the world. I experienced leadership in my own small way at Ma's place because the residents of this household looked up to me for decisions and direction. I realized that when the buck stops at you, you are it. In my case, I was it. The final decision was mine; I could not look for guidance or inspiration outside of me. And there was no external validation coming from anywhere. I needed to have the confidence that I was doing the right thing and that I had done a good job. In any event, I discovered that leadership is a lonely business, not for the faint of heart or the insecure. I realized that I only needed external validation when I had not done enough or my best.

Since I have been taking care of Ma, many elders have blessed me by saying, "You are doing so much *sewa* of your mother; it will bear fruit." I think they meant in a karmic sense. I then started thinking about what constitutes sewa. Sewa is a Hindi word meaning "being of service to others." What does it really mean to be of service to others from the perspective of the service provider? Does one have to inconvenience oneself in some way—physically, emotionally, or financially—for one's efforts to be considered service? If yes, how much inconvenience is sufficient before sewa can bear karmic fruit? What if a wealthy person spends a lot of money that benefits others but their expenditure is not to their financial, emotional, or physical detriment? Would their actions constitute sewa? What if the same rich person, having spent a lot of money in the service of others, also forgoes any tax benefits that they could have reaped? That would not be smart but would be somewhat to their financial detriment. Would it now qualify as sewa? By this logic, could a wealthy person's acts of philanthropy ever be considered sewa? On the other hand, when a poor person gives charity and that action has a significant impact on their financial situation, shouldn't the fruit on their karmic tree be sweeter? What if someone is looking after another and is doing so out of compulsion? Is that sewa? I think the answer perhaps lies in the intention. If one's deed is a selfless act, without regard to personal loss or gain, then possibly the actions amount toward the karmic fruit bearing sewa. If one's actions arise out of thoughts of gain, whether in this world or the next, then I do not think it is a selfless gesture even though others may benefit by such actions. Or am I just frustrated about my circumstances that I want this to be true, that in order to truly serve another, one has to put another's interests above one's own and do so at some level of inconvenience to oneself. If there is no sacrifice, there is no sewa. So, if the primary beneficiary of my actions is me, then my action cannot constitute sewa, even though it may benefit another. This is the kind of thinking that led the sorting hat to send me back to Earth. (See page 57.)

As I go through this challenging phase of my life, I am constantly confronted by my own humanity. I have been thinking about how we relate to our fellow humans' fortunes and misfortunes. I have observed that we are better able to sympathize with others' misfortunes than rejoice with them in their good fortunes. When relating to the misfortunes of others, at some level, we are grateful that it is not us enduring the hardship, the "thank God it's not me" emotion. I believe it is harder to fully rejoice with others in their good fortunes even if our joy for them is authentic, and our intentions to be happy for them are genuine. But sometimes there is a lingering "what about me" syndrome. Or, if this is not so, I have just revealed myself to be a lesser human than others.

I am so alone on my journey. Everyone is alone on their journeys. When on this solitary journey, since the path has gotten a little tougher, why is it that I want others to know how tough it is? What does that serve? I do not know, but the desire to scream this from the rooftops is extraordinarily strong. But no one really cares. I do not think it is that people do not care, but perhaps they too are engrossed in the challenges of their own paths to really have the bandwidth to care about anyone else's struggles. And then slowly as I experience this isolation, my voice gets quieter and ultimately silent. Pretty soon I have nothing left to say. Tears come, and I fight them back. I wish tears would become absent too, just like my words. I guess in writing this I am giving expression to my words, but my voice still remains silent. I see this in Ma. Her voice has become silent, and tears also do not come to her easily anymore. Perhaps she has accepted the fact that life is a solitary journey despite the illusion of companionship. One is lucky if there is another human being who can hold your hand, even if it is for a little time whilst you traverse your own path alone. This is the reality of life. Solitude. I can now understand why so many poets have given expression to the concept of *tanhai* (loneliness) or being *tanha* (lonely). They must have experienced this reality up close and personal. The experience of tanhai is more pronounced during tough times, because during the good times, one is tricked into the illusion of friendship and companionship.

In one of my more pensive moments, I was reflecting back on who my papa was. My father was an amazing man. I lost him too early in life. He was an honest man of uncompromising integrity, and consequently his life choices made his life exceedingly challenging and difficult. I think back and recall a particular expression that Papa used to have. It was a smile. It was a smile, but I knew there was something missing from it. I could not put my finger on it then. Some twenty years later, I caught myself with the same expression. I now know and interpret that expression as one of extreme isolation. Papa was like the ocean, absorbing everything thrown at him and emptying himself into nothing and nowhere. All he could do was smile, and people took that at face value because he was our rock. We never thought he could also need something or could get lonely, sad, or frustrated. Now that I am getting glimpses into life, I wish I had recognized that and been there for him. But at the time, I had not really started to experience life. And I think when life starts to happen, the journey becomes quite solitary. I have been crying since morning. This was a luxury Papa was never allowed.

One day as I was draining Ma's dialysis, I had an insight into the "woe is me" routine and the evolution into silence from peddling one's sob stories. There were several points that became clear to me. First, very few people care that one is going through a rough patch in life. Everyone is busy with their own challenges. Upon hearing the woeful tale, even the ones that do care can only utter well-intentioned, genuine words of sympathy to the effect of "you poor thing." But such words are to no avail, as they cannot better one's situation. Second, some people might even derive comfort at one's plight knowing that they are not alone in experiencing the struggles of life. Third, once life gets really challenging, there comes a point where the fatigue of the everyday battle of life makes one too tired to even attempt to describe one's pain, sorrow, or suffering, and one evolves into a state of dignified silence.

Dear Life,

I am getting a glimpse into how and why people can get silent. Life replaces chatter with silence as there aren't many who share one's experience to understand enough to have a conversation about it. And others simply don't care. I, too, am becoming increasingly silent. No one wants to listen. Everyone wants to talk. Is there any point to conversation? I write because I must express despite the futility of my expression. I write so I may be heard even if it is by an audience of one, me. Am I losing my touch, or am I evolving? Is it that I do not have the skills to converse anymore, or is it that I don't need to have my point of view be accepted?

Questioningly yours,
The Ordinary Human

I have been thinking more about the age-old proverb "silence is golden." When we talk, what do we actually say? Mostly we complain, boast, vent, gossip, preach, etc. Then there is small talk. Is it wasteful? Because neither party in that conversation actually cares about what is being said. How about the question, "How are you?" This is not a question asked to illicit information regarding how one actually is. If one starts to say how one is, one will be met with rolling eyes. When we meet socially, we typically discuss current events, trends, politics, weather, and the like. With respect to politics, social interactions are by and large with like-minded people, so those conversations become like preaching to the choir. Few will see a differing point of view, and fewer still will move from their position. There is value in discussing current events and trends because they may actually be informative. The more I think about it, the more persuaded I am that there are very few instances in which conversation is useful. A couple of instances that come to mind are education and helping a loved one unburden or share in their joy or sorrow. The former must be sought else it becomes preachy. The latter is limited to a small circle of people. Rest, in my humble opinion, is simply whiling away time. It is unproductive, or in some cases, even counterproductive. Having made a case against conversation and in favor of silence, I will now retract from my position and declare that we humans are social creatures. Even if we are more interested in talking than listening and even if most conversation is not useful, it is absolutely essential for our mental and physical well-being to be in the company of others and to hear and be heard. I believe it is a fundamental need of humanity.

To support my previous proposition that humans are social creatures and have a fundamental need for conversation and interaction with other humans, I submit evidence from a seemingly insignificant source. I refer to T-shirts that make statements—political, funny, witty, smart, and so on. My T-shirt today triggered this thought. It states, "I am a writer. I make the voices in my head work for me." Yes, I found it funny, and that is why I am wearing it. But in a grander scheme, I wanted others to interact with the statement, find it funny, ask me about being a writer, or just silently register that this geek is a writer. And my T-shirt did serve the purpose it was intended for, leading to interaction with my fellow humans. Many people, including strangers, commented on it. And many, silently, must have either got a chuckle out of it or judged me favorably or unfavorably. I own many such statement T-shirts, and unfailingly, they lead to interactions with my fellow humans.

One day I had come in from the hundred-degree sweltering heat of a Delhi summer. I chugged a glass of ice-cold water and then rushed to the washroom, having to pee really bad. I am sure many of you can relate to what I am referring to. Sometimes the urge to pee is so intense, and when you get to do it, the relief is one of the most incredible feelings. I was just enjoying this feeling when guilt struck. Ma had stopped producing urine. As she was a dialysis patient, we would never let her chug water. She was only allowed to sip very tiny sips of measured quantities of water. I never knew how much for granted I took these activities until I thought of Ma. I was simultaneously filled with guilt and gratitude.

Gratitude

I have faulty vision
Shouldn't I be grateful I can see?

I get migraines
Shouldn't I be grateful they are not terminal?

I cannot walk without pain
Shouldn't I be grateful I can walk?

I am apart from the love of my life
Shouldn't I be grateful I have a love in my life?

I did not bear children
Shouldn't I be grateful I have the love and affection of so many?

Life has been challenging
Shouldn't I be grateful I am being seasoned by it?

Gratitude gives peace
Shouldn't I be grateful that I have so much to be grateful for?

Dear Life,

As you reveal yourself to me more intimately, two things crystallize for me. First, gratitude is the single most powerful tool to make it through life peacefully. Second, kindness is the single most valuable yet underrated virtue possessed by humankind.

Yours truly,
The Ordinary Human

On one of my visits home to the United States, one day we had invited some friends over for dinner, and they canceled on us. I was upset. Then my internal ears perked up—this does not feel good, so I bet life is trying to teach me something. And indeed it was. When people say they do not have time, it simply means that they have other priorities. It is silly to get upset about something like that. The disconnect is because of expectations. Priorities shift. That is all there is to it. Life goes on. Groups come together; they dissolve. New groups form, and they too shall dissolve. Even though this is sounding preachy, it was an important insight for me. And here is my bottom-line learning from it—I must learn to enjoy and appreciate my friends while it is our time together. But when life moves on, as it inevitably does and will, I should learn to let go gracefully and not make others or myself wrong. Treasure the memories that were created, and try to move on with life. Life is too funny for such big sulks resulting from the core nature of life.

More on "expectations." I believe there is a reason why doing charity work for strangers feels so satisfying: at least in the beginning, with strangers, there are no expectations. However, even charity work ceases to be satisfying as soon as the strangers become familiar and expectations form. These can take the form of either expected appreciation, or rather a lack thereof, or a development of self-importance that is not shared by others.

Dear Life,

I think this time the lesson is focusing on expectations—sneaky and destructive little devils. I have been on my guard, but somehow, very quietly, when I am least expecting it, they sneak in and wreak havoc. I have figured out there are expectations. I have figured out they are sneaky. I have figured out they attack. I have figured out they are destructive. What I am figuring out is how to keep them at bay. It took Buddha a lifetime to figure this out. I should at least give myself several lifetimes to get even close. If I can lengthen the duration between attacks, I shall consider myself successful.

Yours truly,
The Ordinary Human

Today I helped a family member resolve a conflict they were having with someone else, and they ended up feeling better about themselves. I felt good about myself too, but that did not last long. I did not receive the acknowledgment I was expecting. Now I am feeling crappy. I will need to let go in order to feel better. It is enormously amusing that we human beings have the talent to turn a good, warm, happy occurrence into a third-rate soap with much drama and heartache because of our bruised egos. I think in all my recent observations and learnings, it is becoming clear to me that the real culprit in life is ego. "If I can only conquer my ego, I can become a super human being," says the ambitious ego. We are now in the realm of meta-ego.

Dear Life,

Thank you for trying to teach me about letting go, the next lesson after learning about expectations. I say "trying to teach me" because it is not a lesson I have mastered. Once one has identified an unmet expectation, the next step in trying to restore equilibrium is to let go. I have found learning to let go is akin to learning to swim. When I kept wanting to swim, I kept sinking. When I relaxed and stopped trying so hard, one day I noticed that I was swimming and not drowning. I keep wanting to let go of things and thoughts. And the more I think of letting them go, the more to the forefront they come. I guess the secret is to keep trying to not try so hard, and then one day, I will just find that I am doing it, I have let go.

Yours truly,
The Ordinary Human

My previous thought got me thinking about the source of disempowerment. I have observed that anytime I feel loss of power, one or a combination of the following reasons is the culprit. My first go-to culprit is always ego. My ego has been bruised. I was not acknowledged, or credit was not given when I was expecting it. If it is not ego, the next usual suspect is responsibility, or rather, a lack thereof. Either I have not done what I know to be right, or I have not done what I said I would do. The third possible culprit in line is related to the first: my expectations have not been met, and I am disappointed. Another culprit is attachment to a person, thing, idea, or outcome. Moving down the list of usual suspects, another one is that I have made someone wrong so that I can be right. Deep down I know I have done this, but instead of taking responsibility, I continue to make the situation worse by going on justifying my initial action. And finally, there is the "I am not living in the moment" culprit. Either I am regretting something I did or did not do in the past, or I am worrying about the future and what will happen. If I am present in the moment and live in the present, life is invariably manageable and almost always decent. So, to summarize, when I feel loss of power, I look to see if there is a bruised ego, an unmet expectation, an attachment, compromised integrity, or absence from the moment. Any number of variations can be ultimately classified into one of these categories. Once the culprit is identified and I have had a good rant, the next step is to let go—simple in principle but the opposite to implement.

Dear Life,

Every time I feel crappy because of something someone said or did or didn't do, or because I think I failed or made a mess of things, I am finding that if instead of wallowing I start asking myself, "What is the learning in this," I feel less bad. After a while, the little voice with the pointy finger becomes less loud and judgmental, and I feel less victimized. Now if only I could implement this strategy. And I must confess, it takes a really long while to even get to the point where I can remember that I have a strategy, let alone implement it. But on the few occasions that I have remembered, I have succeeded, and it has helped. Thanks for listening.

Yours truly,
The Ordinary Human

Life Is Teaching, and I Am Learning

I am learning that not all challenging times are bad times;
they can even be the best of times.

I am learning that the more I complicate things,
the more complicated they get.

I am learning that sometimes I have to win
by letting others win.

I am learning that when I am committed,
life finds a way of supporting me.

I am learning that when I focus on how unfair life has been,
I miss all opportunities to be grateful.

I am learning that the moment I put myself first,
it is game over.

I am learning that I do not have to be the best,
but I do have to do my best.

I am learning that I can only do what I can do.
I have to let go beyond that.

*I am learning that when I think about exhaustion and fatigue,
I get tired.*

*I am learning that adversities are worthy of my undying
gratitude; they transform me.*

*I am learning that the darkest moment is
the brightest opportunity for growth.*

*I am learning that to be needed is a blessing,
to not need, an even bigger blessing.*

*I am learning that all any one of us wants to do
is to actually make a difference.*

*I am learning that there is a lot of freedom
in not having a choice.*

*I am learning that as soon as life feels bad,
look for the lesson; it is always there.*

Dear Life,

You have been teaching a lot, and I have been learning some. One of my favorite lessons that fills my heart with joy is the lesson that not all challenging times are bad times; they are just tough, and they can even be the best of times. This is one of the more brilliant insights you have gifted me. Taking care of Ma, watching her suffer, and being away from my home has been as challenging as it gets. But this is absolutely one of the best times of my life, to be able to be with her and learn from her—it is the best. But for these challenges, I would never have gotten so much time with my mother before she left me. I love that you have taught me that there is an alternate, empowering way to relate to challenges in life.

Yours joyfully,
The Ordinary Human

One of my favorite quotes is by Maya Angelou. She said, "Courage is the most important of all the virtues, because without courage, you can't practice any virtue consistently." My ma was an epitome of courage and exemplified Angelou's assertion. One day, I was indulging myself in a bout of self-pity, thinking of things back home. While I was gently stroking Ma's aching body, I decided to share with her my most recent upset with someone close to me. The story was about how much I had done for this person and how disappointed I was in them. Ma indulged me for a bit and then decided enough was enough and cut me short. Here was a woman who was completely dependent on me, yet she had the courage and integrity to not mince her words. She just asked me, "Why did you do what you did for this person?" And then she rolled over, leaving me speechless and annoyed. Once I got over being perturbed with Ma's reaction, I was so grateful to her for not indulging my self-pity but rather very bluntly letting me know that it was neither becoming nor helpful. The lesson she taught me was if one does something for another, one should do it because one wants to, with no expectations. Keeping accounts in relationships is not cool. If accounting is to come into the picture, then it is better to not do at all. Even in this weakened state, she was a fine example of good parenting. I am so grateful that I was born to her. I am so grateful for all this time I had with her.

Dear Life,

Just wanted to share an epiphany with you. I was just able to connect two quotes: "The road to hell is paved with good intentions" and Maya Angelou's, "Courage is the most important of all the virtues, because without courage, you cannot practice any other virtue consistently." That would make an unpracticed virtue a good intention.

Yours as always,
The Ordinary Human

One evening I was watching the sun set. It was beautiful. I missed my husband. I wanted to share this beauty with him. Why does sharing a beautiful sunset with someone you love make it even more beautiful? Or said differently, why does a beautiful experience seem incomplete without someone you love to share it with? Why does the presence of a stranger witnessing the same sunset from the same spot not fulfill that desire of a shared experience? I wonder if it is because when we love someone, we want to make them happy. When they are happy, it enhances our happiness. It is like when we experience direct joy; say its value is x. And then we experience the same joy by reason of having made a loved one joyous; its value becomes multiple times x. The thing being experienced does not change; we change.

Dear Life,

Just wanted to update you on the God front. I am still an agnostic, but I have taken to lighting a diya (a small oil lamp) in Ma's temple every morning after my shower. The shower makes me fresh. Folding my hands makes me humble. And lighting the diya brings light into my heart.

Yours,
The Ordinary Human

Dear Life,

I think one of the biggest mistakes we make is that we want to help people in the manner that we want to help them. Not in the manner they need or want to be helped. And when the one being helped is then dissatisfied and the helper does not feel suitably acknowledged or appreciated, we engage in drama. "I did so much for you, and you didn't even . . ." I hope I am doing right by you, Ma.

Yours truly,
The Ordinary Human

Dear Life,

Today are you trying to teach me that feeling the elements, particularly heat, is a state of mind? I am just not getting it. I am a slow learner, I guess. It's close to a hundred degrees, all doors and windows are closed. There is high humidity and no fan or air-conditioning. I am sleeping with Ma. I am sweating like I have never before. Ma is cold.

Wiltingly yours,
The Ordinary Human

While I was taking care of Ma, my husband and I used to grab opportunities whenever we could to see each other and also continue to chip away at our bucket list at the same time. On this particular occasion, we happened to be in Africa when the Indian festival of Rakhi arrived. Rakhi is a celebration of the bonds of love between a brother and sister. The sister ties a thread bracelet on her brother's wrist, and the brother promises to love and protect her. So, on Rakhi one year, my husband and I were in Tanzania, driving from Ngorongoro Crater to the Serengeti when I had one of the most amazing, uplifting life experiences. As it was Rakhi, I was missing my brother very much. We had not been together on Rakhi for decades, having lived in different countries since adulthood. While en route, something broke in the car, and we had to stop to fix it. There was no one else around (other than hidden big cats), and I thought I would use this opportunity to visit the bush toilet. I had just opened the car door and was contemplating squatting discretely somewhere nearby when a small Maasai boy materialized from nowhere. We looked at each other, and without a word being spoken, he extended a homemade bead bracelet to me. Without thinking twice, I extended my arm to him, and he tied this bracelet on my wrist. The impact of this hit me. Just before we stopped to fix the car, I was feeling melancholy with my thoughts on Rakhi and my brother. And as soon as we stopped, from nowhere this boy came to celebrate the festival with me. I felt one with the universe with a very palpable sensation of knowing that no matter what, all is, and will be, well. I cried silent tears of joy; it was a rare feeling. I was overcome with gratitude.

I was cursing myself about something that I should have done. An insight materialized. I discovered that a "should have" or "should not have" is a regret. It has value as a one-time occurrence if I learn from it. If the same "should have" or "should not have" appears again, it is a liability. For example, I should have gone to the gym. I should not have eaten that donut. I should have walked away . . . Life is full of them. By saying "I should have" or "I should not have," I let myself feel bad, feel regret, and feel like I have paid the price for the action, inaction, event, or thought that triggered my "should have" or "should not have," thus relieving me of further responsibility in the matter. I think this is why I keep repeating my "should haves" and "should not haves" and indulging myself. But in the grander scheme of things, these indulgences come at a great cost to me. A "should have" or "should not have" should be a one-time occurrence only. Is that a meta "should have"?

Dear Life,

The more I live, the more I experience, the less I know. Age sixteen was the high point of my wisdom; I knew everything. It has been downhill since.

Sincerely yours,
The Ordinary Human

After spending day after day for months in the waiting room of the oncology department waiting for Ma to complete her radiation therapy, I actually feel sad when I see people smoking, chewing tobacco, or eating pan masala. Pan masala is a type of an addictive blend comprising beetle nut and other substances. There are diseases that we can do nothing about. But there are many that we can prevent. If only we could exert control over ourselves to engage in behaviors that could keep us out of hospitals. Many times, we only think about it when we find ourselves in the waiting room of a hospital. Regret fills us; if only I could turn time back, I would behave more responsibly. There are so many aspects of my own life that could benefit from a dose of such responsibility. But I still do not get the urgency to alter my behavior and act more responsibly for managing myself. Because I am immortal. Death and disease are for those mere mortals waiting in these hospital rooms.

I had been experiencing hair loss due to stress. But after spending hours in the waiting room of the oncology department every single day for over two months, I stopped complaining about my hair loss or even how tired I was all the time. What I was experiencing was trivial compared to what these oncology patients were going through. I think volunteer work in hospitals, particularly in wards for the terminally ill, should be mandated to give life perspective, arrest petty complaints, appreciate the fragility of life, and become present to all that we have and ought to be grateful for.

Dear Life,

You keep chugging along. Sometimes I chug with you. Sometimes I find that you have chugged me along despite my resistance.

Resistingly yours,
The Ordinary Human

Dear Life,

I have observed that when I am sad or overjoyed and moved to tears, I can feel that emotion physically in the cells of my upper body, particularly my arms. Each cell has a distinct sensation that feels like a combination of dull muted pain and being on a roller coaster. I wonder if others feel the same thing.

Yours forever,
The Ordinary Human

Dear Life,

As I mentioned earlier, my husband and I, in an attempt to manage our now long-distance relationship, had periodically started meeting for a few days somewhere in the world. On one such date, I met my husband in Poland for a quick rendezvous. We were at a famous church in Krakow, and I overheard an old lady in the vicinity who bought a very interesting gift for her friend from the church gift shop. She had bought a pack of paper napkins, albeit pretty ones. I was thinking what a strange gift it was to carry for someone all the way from Poland. Then the lady explained to her companion, "All my friends are my age, and we are into purging. We don't want to collect things anymore. I have started giving disposable and perishable gifts." What an insight. Suddenly this gift of paper napkins was so significant, beautiful, and appropriate.

Yours,
The Ordinary Human

Dear Life,

This same church in Poland had a peculiar smell. It smelled musty-like. I think it was the smell of time. Time has a smell. The past smells like this. Perhaps the smell of time in the future will be different, but this is definitely what the past smells like. What a profound experience.

Yours truly,
The Ordinary Human

Dear Life,

I was wondering why sometimes words ring hollow. Then it occurred to me that words without action are meaningless. And action without words is less effective. I believe successful relationships require a delicate balance of words and action, and the proportions of each vary depending on the individuals involved to yield the correct formula.

Yours,
The Ordinary Human

Dear Life,

I have a confession. Every once in a while, I engage in behavior that I am not proud of. I hope I am not alone in this. But regardless, when I try to justify my behavior in order to feel better, I make the situation worse. I don't feel any better, and the relationship at issue is further compromised. I am learning that when I am honest with myself and acknowledge that my behavior was less than stellar, and in conjunction apologize to the other person without expecting an apology in return, equilibrium gets restored very quickly. I feel light.

Yours truly,
The Ordinary Human

Dear Life,

When I see someone who seemingly has it all, I want to ask them what their demons are. I am certain that no one has it all.

Yours truly,
The Ordinary Human

Dear Life,

I have been thinking about philanthropy. Drop by drop, one fills one's vessel over a lifetime. By vessel, I mean a conceptual receptacle that each one of us has within us that we fill with all manner of wealth. Everyone's vessel size is different in terms of how much each of us needs to fill it. Some are satisfied with less, and some need a lot more. But as it nears full or fills, and if we don't give some away, it will overflow. It occurs to me that it's better to be gracious and share before it inelegantly falls and is wasteful. We cannot hold onto what is excess; it has to overflow. This is science. A receptacle cannot hold more than its size.

Yours truly,
The Ordinary Human

Dear Life,

*Can I ask you a question? I was thinking that I have
a lot of thoughts. A lot of these are weird. There is
never a dull moment in my head. Am I the only one
who has such weird thoughts? I did not want to ask
anyone else lest I reveal my weirdness and find out
that, indeed, I am the only one.*

Yours truly,
The Ordinary Human

Taking care of Ma was a decision that my husband and I had made together. But when I actually started to take care of her and came face-to-face with all the emotional and physical challenges, on occasion, I would feel like life had shoved me into these incredibly challenging circumstances, and I would feel victimized by life. When I would think and say I had no choice, I found that it was a reaction to whatever I was going through, and I found I had no power. Then I realized that every single time I experienced such loss of power, I would have to remind myself that I was with Ma because I chose to be with her and what a privilege it was. Instantaneously, I felt empowered and was able to move forward. I had to choose my then–present life. I took away the permission to engage in futile thoughts such as, "I wish I was here or there, doing this or that." I had to remind myself of my choices and my commitment of seeing Ma through, no matter the length of commitment, no matter the consequences. Sometimes I had to renew my vows several times a day.

Resignation, acceptance, and choice—all three describe a state where no further action will be taken by the person to change the status quo. However, the difference between the mental states in each of these is enormous. Resignation is a completely disempowered state with a sense of helplessness and victimization. In acceptance, there is a bit more empowerment because there is an attempt to try to move forward despite a lack of action to change status quo. For choice, regardless of the difficult circumstances, if one intentionally chooses that circumstance even though there is nothing else to choose, suddenly one is in control and no longer a victim of circumstances. It's an empowered state from which to move forward. I recognize that I have been existing in a state of resignation. There is no magic to making a choice. It is a simple matter of choosing. I declare that in this moment, I choose to be here with Ma, not because I have to, but because I choose to. I further choose to be away from my home and be here and do the best that I possibly can. I do so choose and do so declare.

Dear Life,

What sort of a test is this? There is no training, no curriculum, no syllabus, no time to prepare, no start date, no end date. No results!

Painfully lost,
The Ordinary Human

Dear Life,

I am struggling and lost. You are testing me, and I have no answers. They say that the master will appear when the pupil is ready. I am ready! Where is the master? Ah, I see, you are the master who is teaching and testing at the same time. Regardless of whether I pass or fail, these tests and lessons are designed to teach. Little incidents carrying big lessons.

Gratefully yours,
The Ordinary Human

Life Is Teaching, and I Am Learning, Part II

What is life trying to teach me?

Learn to stay in the moment.

Do not compare yourself to others.

There is no substitute for hard work.

You may be able to fool others but not yourself.

Wishful thinking is a waste of time.

Regrets are a waste of time.

Death is inevitable.

You can only do your best and no more.

Guilt does not substitute for responsibility.

Jealousy and anger are toxic.

Everyone has their own cross to bear. You cannot carry theirs for them.

The ostrich strategy of burying your head in the sand does not work.

If you are not your word, you are nothing.

That is a tough curriculum. I hope I make it.

Dear Life,

*Since you started testing me, I seem to be failing.
How do I rise above it? Either I rise above it or fall
and burn. That is the only grade. A fall from grace
into a deep abyss from which there is no return. I
am close to the point of no return.*

*Failingly yours,
The Ordinary Human*

Dear Life,

Today my mind hurts, and my body aches. I want to tell someone. I want someone to say, "You poor thing." There is no one. Plus, what good will it do? Why this need for pity? Am I alone in this need? I want to sleep for an entire day, preferably without feeling guilt. Does not seem possible with or without guilt.

Looking forward to your response,
The Ordinary Human

As a strategy for survival during this incredibly challenging phase of my life, I defined certain lofty goals "for my sake." These were by no means original or unique to me. However, my having personally experienced a need for them to get me through life made them my own. I have never succeeded in mastering any of them for any measurable length of time. But I was able to conserve some much-needed energy by just keeping them in focus, which in itself was a huge help.

For My Sake

*For my sake, may I do my best and understand
that that is all I can do.*

*For my sake, may I focus only on my karma;
others' karma is none of my business.*

*For my sake, may I be in control
of my own emotions and reactions.*

*For my sake, may I not be the center of my focus;
it is not always about me.*

*For my sake, may I be able to look myself in the mirror
every single day.*

*For my sake, may I be courageous and have the courage
of my convictions.*

*For my sake, may I forgive myself and others,
let things go, and not judge.*

*For my sake, may I be patient, disciplined,
kind, and compassionate.*

*For my sake, may I learn from my mistakes
and be a better person today than I was yesterday.*

Dear Life,

I have been told that dumping baggage at the end of the day is prudent. As I lie down to fall asleep each night, I try to forgive others, and more importantly, myself. Some days I succeed.

Yours, but still lost,
The Ordinary Human

GETS REALLY CHALLENGING

This (her illness and suffering) was her cross to bear. My cross to bear was watching her having to bear her cross.

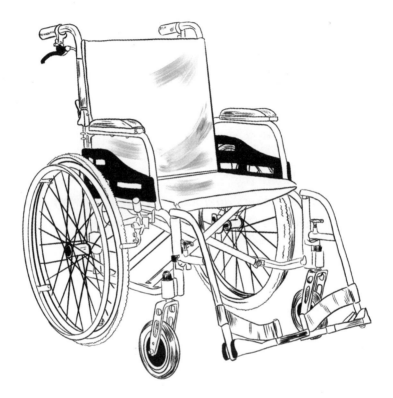

Dear Life,

The next, more-challenging phase has commenced. We have shifted downstairs, as Ma could no longer manage the stairs. A couple of wheelchairs, one with an inbuilt potty, have come to the house. I thought I would update you and prepare you for what's to come.

With fear in my heart,
The Ordinary Human

I am committed to looking after Ma, no matter the costs. This is not a cost-benefit analysis, for the benefits decidedly outweigh the costs. But talking about costs, until now they have been financial, physical, and emotional, and my husband and I have been managing. Now comes the real test. As more time passes, will our relationship withstand the challenges of our unique circumstances? The heaviest of costs indeed. Will I survive this? Will my relationship survive this? I do not know—time will tell. We would not have been able to live with ourselves if we weren't there for Ma. We love each other, and we love Ma. Yet, sometimes, circumstances make us angry, and our humanity gets the better of our intentions. I know we both chose this, yet what I have asked of him is so much bigger than what he has ever asked of me. In any event, it is what it is. We will either make it, or we will not. Regardless of how things turn out, I will forever be in your debt, my friend, for I do not know how I can ever repay your love and generosity to me and my family; thus I shall remain indebted to you. Thank you for being my life partner, and I hope that we will remain friends until this game called life concludes.

Dear Life,

My previous thought, "I will forever be in your debt," inspired an insight. A very interesting sentence. Often used in the English language to emphasize the gratitude one feels at having been helped. It implies a person burdened by an obligation or debt of some sort to the obligee or the creditor. It confirms the existence of a debt. However, upon closer inspection, the very words of the promise prevent the debtor from ever repaying the debt because the moment the debt is repaid, the debtor violates his promise of forever being in the creditor's debt. It is, in fact, a promise to never repay the debt. What a unique sentiment!

Bemusedly yours,
The Ordinary Human

I am an agnostic. I do not know about God. But I believe in the power of the Universe. Repeatedly the Universe has delivered. Requests need to be specific. It requires that one do one's homework. Know what one wants. Random requests, such as make me happy or give me a job, are too vague; the Universe has no clue what to do with such ambiguity. The Universe is not vindictive; it just does not know how and what to deliver. The moment the request becomes specific, in no time, the almighty and giving Universe delivers. It loves us all equally. It does not like negative requests. It is not a personal genie; it will not cause harm to another at one's request. I am not its master. I am one with it.

One of my favorite quotes is by Scottish mountaineer and writer W. H. Murray: "Until one is committed, there is hesitancy, the chance to draw back, always ineffectiveness. [But] the moment one definitely commits oneself, then providence moves too." I had gone home to the United States for a couple of weeks, and upon arriving back in India, I found that Ma could barely walk now, and going down the stairs had become insurmountable. She had a doctor's appointment and had to be carried down and back up in a chair; it was not safe for her or anyone. Ma's house had a ground floor, but it was unlivable. We neither had the time nor the manpower to manage a renovation project. The only solution I could think of was that we needed a lift. After exploring a bit, the only affordable and viable option that emerged was an industrial hydraulic lift that would be sufficient for a wheelchair and an attendant. It was an inelegant and expensive solution, but it was still a solution. I was pretty dejected. I can only describe what happened next as divine intervention with providence stepping in. I, out of the blue, thought of a high school friend whom I had not met or spoken to in thirty-five years. I had heard that he had become a big businessman, and I called him thinking he may be able to connect me to a lift guy. After I explained our situation, instead of connecting me to a lift guy, he said, "Shift downstairs." He told me that he was in construction, and that for the cost of an industrial lift, he would renovate my entire downstairs and make it like new in ten days. My initial reaction was that this was just talk, because that is not possible in the US, let alone India. He called me the next morning and informed me that he was on his way with his best construction supervisor. They looked and confirmed the duration and budget and that they would have a proposal within a day and finish in ten days. I was still skeptical. He called the next day and informed me that all construction plans were complete, and a team of ten would be there the following day. My friend delivered as promised. Within two weeks of our initial conversation, we had shifted downstairs with little or no inconvenience to me. My friend told me, "You are taking care of your mother. This is my contribution to the care of a parent." I am in awe of my friend, bowed in gratitude to him and the Universe, and humbled by how all this transpired in such a brief time, all seemingly effortlessly. Murray was right. The only thing I had brought to the table was my commitment to caring for Ma, and providence moved too.

M a was not doing great. I remained hopeful, but it was quite tough. Even during those challenging times, interesting life-affirming anecdotes continued to occur. Here is one that I am calling "A Debt Repaid." Several years ago, a housecleaner used to work for Ma. She was young and pregnant. Ma would not let her lift anything or do anything. Ma would make Omi, her attendant and companion, help her as much as she needed. The baby she was carrying went on to become a nurse, and this nurse came to our house yesterday under very urgent medical circumstances and took amazing care of Ma. Even in these very tense circumstances, I felt the warm fuzzies when Omi told me who this young nurse was.

I have been feeling overwhelmed and at times only able to function with enormous effort. In addition to all Ma's attendants being sick, failure of mom's dialysis machine, a burst water pipe in the house, and a sudden cockroach infestation, the most significant source of our stress is coming from the fact that Omi's married daughter and her one-year-old girl have been missing for a week. No one knows what may have happened to them. My heart just breaks for him. I want to share an anecdote from this morning that parted the dark clouds just a tiny bit; I felt a tiny ray of warmth and sunshine. As everyone at home is sick, I am on the morning milk, bread, and eggs duty. Given how disturbed we all were, once I got to the shop, I discovered I had forgotten my money pouch. I told the guy I had forgotten money and that I would be right back. The guy was so nice and insisted that I take the milk and bread and pay him the next day. I was quite touched by this gesture and told him that I did need to go back and get money because I needed to buy other things as well. At this point, the guy took out a two-hundred-rupee note and told me to finish all my chores for the morning and return the money to him the next day. I was blown away by this. I interpreted the events of the morning as a message from the Universe telling me to hang in there and that all will work itself out. Experiences like this restore one's faith in humanity. What really moved and inspired me about this gentleman's actions was that *he* was genuinely grateful for the opportunity to be able to help someone in need. A small experience with a significant impact.

End of the day has come. Pretty tough day. I need to get tougher. It distresses me so to see Ma suffering, to the extent it saps me of my energies. I need to be there for her. I need to witness her pain and not let it consume me. I need to care for her, love her, and be enormously patient. I cannot let her pain become my pain because then I become ineffective. I need to recognize her pain and be there for her, but I cannot have her pain become me. Tomorrow will be better. I love you, Ma.

This (her illness and suffering) was her cross to bear. My cross to bear was watching her having to bear her cross. Very painful. If only I could separate my attachment from what I needed to do. I would often find myself crying out, "Universe, please help! Give me strength."

I evolved as a caregiver over the period of five years that I cared for Ma. One of my more insightful insights was that the cure cannot be worse than the disease. When I started caring for Ma, she was very alert and normal in every way, other than the fact of her disease and the necessary care for it. I was a firm caregiver, and Ma surrendered to me completely. She placed her life in my hands. She loved food, and we put her on a strict diet. One morning as I consumed an entire bowl of nuts, one of Ma's favorite things, I remembered that I would give her two cashews and two almonds, no more because they were not good for her. Then as time went on, her health deteriorated to a point where she could not eat anything. At this point it dawned on me that the cure was worse than the disease. I took all rules off the table. And in 2020, the last year of her life, I begged her to eat anything that her heart desired. And her heart desired nothing. I hope and pray that I did right by her. I love you, Ma. Please forgive me if I made the last few years of your life harder than they should have been.

Dear Life,

The pain is inside me.

Therefore, it cannot be bigger than me, can it?

Trying to make it,
The Ordinary Human

Dear Life,

I need a change of residence. I have been living in my head for longer than is healthy, playing and replaying actual and imagined events over and over again. I am exhausted and need fresh air.

Yours,
The Ordinary Human

Sometimes my days got so challenging that all I wanted to do was whine and lay responsibility elsewhere. For a few moments, it could make me feel better. But as soon as the rant was done, I found I had lost more energy and felt worse. The insight for me was that I needed to focus on what I could do and not on what others had not done. Not because I was a better person but because I just did not have the extra bandwidth to waste energy given everything else I had to manage. When I only focused on what I could do, I was more productive, less tired, and in general less angry and happier.

Dear Life,

You feel insurmountable right now. There is no respite in sight. In this moment it feels like the only way it will be okay will be one day when I rest forever, engulfed in a warm blanket of flames. I know this feeling will pass; I have to believe that. I wanted to lighten my load by sharing it with you.

Yours, but struggling,
The Ordinary Human

Dear Life,

I had a vision of sitting in my favorite chair at home, facing the fireplace with my feet up, holding a glass of a delicious red, nibbling on my favorite Maytag blue cheese. I sighed deeply and did a heavy load of guilt. It makes me sad that my life has changed. It makes me sad that when I want that, by default I don't want this. Ma relies on me one hundred percent and has entrusted her life into my hands. Instead of being grateful for this privilege and this enormous responsibility, I want a glass of wine?

Guilt ridden and yours,
The Ordinary Human

Dear Life,

I love today's lesson! I have discovered something interesting about guilt. If I do what I know I need to do, guilt does not arise. There may be disappointment or sadness, but there is no room for guilt. I experience guilt as a mechanism to substitute for responsibility by making myself feel bad. By feeling bad, I feel as though I have acted sufficient to the extent that I no longer have to be responsible. Guilt substitutes for responsibility. In that sense, it is like righteous indignation.

Always yours,
The Ordinary Human

I had heard about boot camp. This phase of my life felt like I was in one. I had heard how hard it was and how individuals rose above themselves and accomplished things that they thought were beyond their reach. I was in that misery stage where every moment felt like a failure and success, unattainable. But I was convinced that if I just did not give up and got up every time I fell, I would come out the other end with eyes that shone with discipline, determination, courage, strength, and the pride of having achieved what seemed impossible. I was not going to give up even though the goal seemed distant and unattainable.

One day I wrote, "I hope Ma does not mistake my expressions of fatigue and exhaustion for burden. She is not a burden on me. It truly is a privilege to care for her. But I am physically, mentally, and emotionally exhausted. These are my human limitations. I have to replenish my heart so that I have something to give. I feel bankrupt right now."

There were days when I said to myself, "Today I do not want to do this." I am angry that I cannot even wish for anything different, for my life to normalize. Because the only way that will happen is not the outcome I want. What am I to do? How am I to get through this? For what am I allowed to wish? All that I know to be counterproductive, I want to indulge in today. I want to compare my life to others and scream from a mountaintop, "Is this fair?" But at the end of the day, after allowing myself a small indulgence of self-pity, I will have to take charge lest I cross the point of no return. I hate today. I ask for help; none is coming. No one but me can help. I hate that I have to be responsible. I hate that no one has any idea of what I am going through. Only I can stop this destructive thinking and help myself. I do not think I am there yet. Maybe another hour's indulgence. Today I cannot stop the tears, I cannot stop the sadness, I cannot stop the ache. I cannot wish for a change. I will stay with this until it changes. I will do this because I am here for Ma.

A nger is so toxic; it has made me physically and emotionally ill. It has not affected the recipients of my wrath, not even a tiny bit. They do not even know. Indulging in this self-indulgence is expensive. I must stop it. The cost is just too high. Plus, it is heavy on resources—it takes a great deal to pull oneself out of the depths of despair. In addition, more resources are required to fix all the damage caused by one's actions and behavior while in the self-indulgent state. Some damage is even beyond repair, particularly in the area of relationships.

Dear Life,

Is today's lesson about anger? The overall loss of control is making me experience extreme anger and rage. But I am grateful, for I could not have conquered anger until I knew and felt it. I am knowing it and feeling it now. I think conquering it is an unrealistic goal, but at least now there is a possibility that I shall be able to manage it. It is certainly a worthy adversary.

Yours,
The Ordinary Human

I had been so down in the dumps that once when I went to see mom's doctor, she prescribed me an antidepressant because I had an emotional meltdown in her office. I had been telling myself, "One kind word from anyone and I will go to pieces." There were no kind words, just an absence of rudeness, and that was sufficient kindness to precipitate my meltdown. She told me I was experiencing caregiver burnout. I was. Life was bloody tough. As I brooded over how tough life was, suddenly and unexpectedly a ray of positivity hit me, and I perked up. It occurred to me that this was an opportunity for me to grow as a human being. It was a very defining moment in my life. I would either crash and burn or emerge stronger. I did not have any intention of crashing and burning. Not because I was arrogant that I could make it, but because the incentive for making it was very compelling. I wanted to be there for Ma. Every time I started to break down, I remembered my father quoting Swami Vivekananda: "What is needed are muscles of iron and nerves of steel." At the time, I seemed to be composed of muscles and nerves of marshmallows.

One day I wrote, "Ma has not been keeping too well. Omi is completely stretched and overburdened but takes care of her with love and complete commitment and responsibility. He is inspiring. Ma acknowledges this fact. I too desire acknowledgment. I do not know if anyone sees, but my life has completely changed. I quit my job, risked my relationship, and put our financial security on the line. All this effort seems invisible. Why am I so human? Why this desire for acknowledgment? Why do I have to remind myself that I am doing all this because I have chosen to do so? I know my life is exactly how it is because it is a sum total of all the choices I have made. I am responsible. I would not change anything other than the desire for acknowledgment. My failings continually introduce me to my humanity."

THE BEGINNING OF THE END

I thought watching you suffer and in pain was the toughest thing I have ever had to do. But it was dwarfed by my loss of you, which I thought had to be the toughest thing I have ever had to endure. I have been proven wrong again. Trying to move forward while managing my grief seems insurmountable. You taught me everything I needed to know in order to survive. You even showed me how to die. But your colossal failure—you failed to teach me how to live without you.

I was optimistic for the new year. That as soon as this horrid 2019 was over, somehow, magically, everything would be fine. It proved not to be so. As the new year set in, Ma experienced a steep decline. January 1, 2020, started with her throwing up and not being able to retain anything. We were giving her injection upon injection of various medications to try to make her feel better. I called my brother in a soggy mess. He tried to reassure me by telling me that everything would be fine. It would be how it would be, and I had to deal with that. I was not fine with it, but I still had to deal with it. This was truly not how I had envisioned 2020 starting. This was where hope came in—when there was no control.

When Ma's health started to take a serious dive, my thoughts turned to the concept of hope, and I wrote, "I have been thinking about the concept of hope a lot lately. It is an interesting word. Most of us think of it as a positive thing. In reality, it is the love child of despair and gloom. Hope is only born in distressing times. If all is well, then hope neither has to nor does actually exist. There is a place for hope in sickness, death, and misfortune. And once it comes into existence, it has the capacity to go on to do remarkable things. But the fact of the matter is, "hope" comes into play only when all is lost. There are no more actions to be taken. There is no control. There is nothing more to be done other than to hope. But once hope kicks in, it can show one a way to move forward in the face of complete loss of control. I hope I am doing right by you, Ma."

Dear Life,

For me, hope is one of the scariest words. Ma is not doing well; I am hopeful and scared. I hope she gets better. I am scared because hope is all I have.

Hopefully yours,
The Ordinary Human

We are only two siblings—my brother and me. Ma had a special spot for each of us in her heart. Ma sometimes really missed my brother. He had his place in Ma's heart, and no matter what, I could not fulfill the longing she felt for him. One time Ma was really sick and missing my brother a lot. I lost it and got mad with him. I was completely taken aback by what my ma had to say at my outburst. Never having been a mother myself, I was shocked that she was not upset that she had not heard from my brother in a few days. She was upset that because she had not heard from him, she had no way of knowing that her baby was doing okay. I was humbled into silence. I think a mother-and-child relationship is perhaps the only relationship where a mother is able to step outside of herself and genuinely have a circumstance be about her child. I believe many fathers can do that too. But otherwise, my observation has been that it is always about us, myself included, in this less-than-flattering assessment of humanity.

I was wondering if when things are difficult, is there a self-destructive force that sort of propels one to do, say, and think things that will make one's life more difficult? Am I alone in sensing this? It takes real effort to resist the temptation to not self-destruct. It is difficult to grasp that if I cannot do anything to make things better, I should do nothing. I think this must be the answer. It is hard to not act. In difficult situations, sometimes the best course of action is inaction. But taking no action is intuitively inadequate. Therefore, we feel compelled to do something and then end up making things worse. I am just sitting here. I do not know how to make things better. I am battling the urge to do stuff that I know will make things worse. So I am writing this thought in my little phone.

Dear Bony,

Your presence here since March 12, 2020, is not a mere coincidence or happenstance. You are my husband's nephew, but you were sent here by some divine design to see Ma through. I am unable to articulate what your connection to her was or to me is. But there is no doubt that there is some higher-level design at play in this human drama. The date on which you arrived was so precise to ensure your presence here in Delhi. However, even if we were not in lockdown because of COVID-19, you are the type of person who would have stayed on to help us through this difficult journey because that is who you are. Words often seem insufficient to express the intensity of one's feelings. I am so grateful for you—grateful for the soul that resides in you. Ma saw Jesus Christ in you, and I trust her instincts. There is something very spiritual about you. You will say, "It's his grace." And it is. That is what makes it spiritual.

With love and gratitude,
Your kaki (aunt)

I had not written in a while. Ma had been on and off intravenous fluids and drugs for four months. Every once in a while she seemed to have a good day, but I knew she was getting lost somewhere. Her mind was slowly getting foggy. I would stay up all night with her because she could not turn sides by herself anymore. She would also be in a lot of pain and extremely uncomfortable all night, catching only a few minutes of sleep here and there out of sheer fatigue. Once dawn broke, Omi would take over, and I would sleep the first half of the day. One day after completing my night shift, when I was sleeping, Ma was crying; she thought that I had fallen and hurt myself. Omi woke me up and I came to her, and she kissed me and kissed me and could not stop loving me. Later in the day, I put my hand next to her lips expecting kisses, but she closed her lips and turned over and gave Omi a big hug and many kisses. He deserved it for sure, but it was very painful for me because I thought she was angry with me. I am just guessing, but I wonder if she ever thought me responsible for her pain and suffering because I was the one making all the decisions, and each of those decisions would always be a cause of significant physical pain for her in terms of medical treatment. The learning and the test for me seemed to be the conviction of my commitment. Was it unwavering in the face of moments like this? I so hoped it was. I would mutter to myself, "No matter what, no matter how hard, I will see you through, Ma. I love you."

It filled my heart with dread that the only things sustaining Ma, a dialysis patient, were fluids and medicines, which we were administering intravenously. She had stopped consuming anything orally. We were artificially hydrating and artificially dehydrating Ma's body. I could not tell her this, but I would often think while looking at her, hoping that somehow I could communicate this to her telepathically, "You don't know how much it hurts me to see you suffer and how helpless I feel when I can't help you feel better. No matter how hard this journey gets, I am with you all the way unless God calls me before he does you."

Dear Life,

Today I just want to sit and cry. I have done that. It has not helped. I want to scream and break things. I suspect that will not help either. Perhaps writing to you will.

Grateful for your ear,
The Ordinary Human

As Ma got worse, I felt so overwhelmed and was drowning in feelings of despair. The only thing I could do at the time was to learn to just stay with those feelings. Acknowledge the feelings but not fight to change them. The battle I needed to be fighting was the battle to move forward despite the burdensome feelings. If I fought to change the feelings and also fought to move forward, I ended up fighting two battles, and my effort to try to move forward got diluted. I learned that feelings were temporary. They changed constantly. I needed to just acknowledge their existence and try to move past them.

Dear Life,

Is it too much to ask to be permitted to exit on my own terms? They say suicide is a coward's way out. I hope when the time comes, I will have the courage to be a coward.

As always yours,
The Ordinary Human

Dear Life,

I think death is the ultimate FOMO—fear of missing out.

Yours truly,
The Ordinary Human

Dear Death,

May my ma live every single day of life that has been allocated for her in peace, happiness, and comfort. When her days are done, please be kind. Let her never find out that you came for her and took her. May her passing be so silent and secretive that she neither hears it coming nor ever discovers it happened.

Humbly yours,
The Ordinary Human

Dear Life,

Please don't misunderstand me, but I need to unburden myself. Today I feel like I am being punished. Ma has lost all sense of herself, anyone else, and time. I have been up all night. Even before my head hits the pillow, she starts crying, and I need to comfort her. I know she is in a lot of pain. I am experiencing extreme caregiver burnout. My emotional electrolytes are completely out of whack. There is a lot of ground left in this marathon, and I need to replenish myself. But I don't know how to do that. So, help me, please!

Desperately yours,
The Ordinary Human

Dear Chand,

Thank you for helping me take care of Ma. I run my analyses and decisions by you, of course, for your medical expertise, but also so you can keep me honest regarding my decisions. They need to be motivated by what's best for Ma and not by the level of ease or difficulty for me in implementing the chosen course of action.

Forever in your debt,
Your sister-in-law

Dear Anil, Kishen, Yoginder, Deepak, Gautam, and Amit,

My undying gratitude to you all for taking such good care of my mother. Anil, you moved heaven and earth in the very difficult time of COVID-19 to get Ma the medications she needed. Kishen and Yoginder, you were her nurses, but you cared for her as your own mother. Deepak, Gautam, and Amit, you looked after my mother as your own grandmother. She too cared for all of you as her sons and grandsons. May all your karmic accounts be credited for all the good deeds you did while you were with us.

With much gratitude,
Your didi (older sister) and buaji (aunt)

Just when I thought things could not get tougher, they did. Ma was struggling for her life. I felt like it was my fault. If I had cared for her better, she would not be struggling so much. I can honestly say that I tried my best, but my best was insufficient. Ma was in a lot of pain; she was frustrated, and I am sure she was afraid as well. She was angry with me. I had to keep my own emotions at bay and be the caregiver I needed to be because Ma needed me the most then. And it was the most difficult thing for me to do. It was difficult on so many levels. I was trying to figure out the correct and best medical care while trying to keep my focus on the fact that it was about her and not me. Ma had always been an amazingly easy patient to take care of, a pleasure. She never complained, always cooperated, and kept herself in good spirits. But I think as her time drew near, I did not know what her mind, body, and soul were experiencing. She was also not entirely coherent. On occasion, I felt like she was shunning me. Maybe because I was the decision maker, and all her pain could be attributed to all my decisions. Every day and sometimes every moment, I would pray for help—help from whom, I knew not, but help to help me do what I was committed to doing, to see Ma through. I knew Ma did not mean to be angry toward me. I knew she was scared and in pain. I hoped she would exit with fond memories of me, not as the person responsible for making her suffer.

I did not know how long I had her for. It may have been hours or days, but I knew we were reaching the end of the game soon. She brought me into the world. She was in labor when she brought me into the world. She was in pain, but it was a labor of joy. I was in labor of exit, and it was a labor of pain and grief. She held my hand, watched me get stronger, and let go when it was time. I was holding her hand, watching her get weaker, and helping her exit. I knew I would have to let go of her hand when it was time. There was pride and joy in her letting go. There was sadness and permanence in my letting go. I thanked Ma for giving me life, and I hoped silently that when she left, she would find peace and joy.

Four days before Ma left us was an exceedingly difficult day. We almost lost her on the seventh of May. Her eyes were not moving, and she was not responding. I thought the time had come, and I wanted her to go in peace. Yet I was not ready to let go of her. I kept saying to her, "Ma, it's okay, you can let go." With my sister-in-law's help, we had created a mini makeshift ICU setup at home in anticipation of this moment. We had two nurses. We called my sister-in-law in Kolkata, and she instructed us as to what emergency injections to administer. While holding her, I kept telling her it was okay for her to let go while we pummeled her with needles in an attempt to keep her alive. I was giving her mixed messages. We had my husband in the US, my brother in Botswana, and his older son in Australia on the phone so they could also be with her in her last moments. I do not know what they must have thought of my encouragement for Ma to let go, but it came from a place of not wanting her to suffer anymore. It was from a place of not wanting to watch her suffer anymore. Yet we kept administering medication to try to keep her alive. She somehow pulled through and was with us for four more days after this. I think she did not go on the seventh because it was not elegant. There were too many of us around her and each of us, out of our own hysterics, was yelling different things. When she finally did leave on the eleventh, it was a quiet, peaceful, elegant, and graceful exit.

Dear Life,

May 10, 2020, was the day before Ma left me forever. She was withdrawn. She was just not engaging with me. And out of sadness, I started writing in my journal. I wrote in Hindi, "Shayad meri sewa main koi kami rah gayi. Mujhe maaf kar dena meri Ma." I had written, "Perhaps I was deficient in my care of you. Please forgive me, Ma." She saw me writing and gestured to me to come to her. She placed her hand on my head and blessed me and said, "Tu likh"—you write. Her last words to me ever. Her last words to anyone ever.

Bowed in humility and gratitude,
The Ordinary Human

I could tell that things were getting worse. On the morning of the eleventh, I talked to as many nephrologists as I could. I could not go see anyone because we were in COVID lockdown. None of the doctors had anything encouraging to say. I had been up the entire previous night and by afternoon was emotionally and physically drained and exhausted. I slept for a bit and woke up in the evening. Before going to see Ma, I went to the kitchen to organize dinner, when her nurse came and said to me with some urgency, "Ma'am, please come, Ma doesn't look right." I rushed. I sat next to her and held her hand and kept calling to her softly. There were no sounds other than my silent sobbing because I knew that it was time. I just held her hand for about ten minutes, after which her eyes become fixed; she looked to be at peace, and the nurse placed a stethoscope on her chest and declared that Ma had left. Very quietly, very peacefully, and with much dignity, my ma had left me. I had been expecting this moment for a while, but I found myself completely unprepared. I was not prepared for the emptiness and loss I felt. From that moment on, my ma had become a memory, and I had become an orphan.

Dear Ma,

When you died, I thought and expected that when free from the physical limitations of your body, you would come and bless me. Your soul would have supernatural powers, and you would just make everything okay and great in my life. But not only are things not great, I find myself struggling. Where are you, Ma?

Struggling and lost,
Your daughter

Dear Ma,

With you gone, I have no one I can utter these words to. I have no one I can share these thoughts with. No one to tell me lies that I am special, although for you this was not a lie. I was special. I miss you. I need you. Where did you go?

Lost without you,
Your daughter

REENTRY

My absence from my universe as I knew it had led to a vanishing of me from it. I came back and struggled to find my place in my own universe. The void I had left had quickly filled with other things and other people.

Feel like crap. Every external validation has failed. Internal validation is not working. Need strength, miracles, self-care, and gratitude. Everyone has moved on. Patience is wearing thin. I am unable to explain why I am feeling so much guilt and still feeling so much grief. Ma was eighty-five, and I am fifty-five. Neither of us young. I should be able to move on. But I haven't . . . Am I just using it as a crutch for not being responsible and moving forward? Are all my aches and pains psychosomatic? I do not know. I hope not.

Today it is a month since Ma left. What am I feeling? I miss Ma, but do I miss her as much as I thought I would? Is it because the relief of not watching her suffer so much outweighs her absence? Is it that I have had time to overcome the physical fatigue and exhaustion? I miss you, Ma, but I feel so guilty that I seem to be doing okay. I laugh, I eat, I sleep, I play. I wish you were with me to enjoy all those things like you used to when you were not ill. I hope you are okay wherever you are and that the passing from this life to wherever you went was not painful. I love you more than you will ever know. I hope I never made you feel like a burden, and if on some occasion my fatigue made my humanity come through, I hope you forgave me. I love you, my ma.

In love there is no accounting. Ma loved us because we were her children. But on occasion, she felt guilty that because of her, our lives were inconvenienced. Your soul should feel no obligation to us, monetary or otherwise. Be free, Ma. You owe your children nothing. We owe you for the life you gave us, for the love and nurturing. I, on the other hand, will forever remain in your debt. I can never forget what you have done for me and my family. I can never repay your kindness and generosity. Nor do I want to. If I remain indebted to you, I will have to encounter you for lifetimes to come. For neither can I repay, nor do I want to. This is my assurance that you and I shall meet every single lifetime, where I can attempt to repay you unsuccessfully.

When I was taking care of Ma, I received so many blessings from so many people. The gist of all of them was that you have taken care of your mother, God will take care of you. Ma left. I returned to the US. Not only did I not feel cared for by God, but I felt abandoned. Health was a mess, professional life was a mess, relationships needed work. I guess what all those blessings had that I did not see or read was a fine print. God will take care of you so long as you take care of yourself. I was thinking that I have put in a lot of hard work with a lot of love and integrity, and I was hoping to cash in on it from the Karma Bank of Humans and Humanity. I am figuring out that there are only deposits—not sure where the withdrawals are.

I had the most amazing insight to be able to move forward. When sometimes I felt angry or frustrated while taking care of my ma, it was merely an expression of physical fatigue and exhaustion. It was never, and could never have been, a reflection of anger with her. How could it? I loved her, completely and unconditionally. I still do. That anger never brought into question the intensity of my love for her. It was a displeasure expressed in the form of anger for having physical limitations of my human body in taking care of her. I have been struggling with this and feeling guilty, but I feel somewhat unburdened with this insight. No one could have or can love my ma more than I did or do. I am grateful for the privilege of having been able to take care of her. I had been incorrectly equating my loss of control on occasion to a diminution of love for her. That is simply not the case; it is an impossibility. And I am also relieved that those occasions were few and far between. I love you, Ma, and I am sorry for those moments of loss of control, but just know that I loved you more than you could ever imagine.

We attach such significance to dates and anniversaries. Today is a year since Ma left me. I do not understand how this happened. I do not understand that of the 365 days that have passed without you on this earth, each day has been so heavy and burdensome. Yet, in the blink of an eye, an entire year has gone by. In some respects, it just feels like another day. Yet it is a significant day. I do not get why it should be so significant. You have gone, and every single day that has passed and every single day that will come will be a day with no you. I find birthdays and anniversaries disappointing. They are just another day. I feel I have to generate the excitement or sadness to make them special or significant. Is it that I am weird? No, I think it is because I am incredibly lucky that I have felt loved every single day, and every day has been special in my life. And I do not need a significant day to remind me that you are gone, for I miss you so very much every single day. So a day that marks the completion of a revolution around the sun is precisely that. No more, no less. I am unable to miss Ma more today because I miss her intensely every day. I wish I still had your hand over my head—blessing me, loving me, and protecting me. I will have to be content with your words and thoughts, the memory of your laughter, and the image of your smile, which are with me today and always. I hope you are at peace and happy wherever you are, my dearest ma. I feel liberated from the constraints of special and significant days to remember and celebrate you every single day.

India is so strange. So exasperating. How can a place so frustrating be so endearing? I left India when I was barely out of my teens. And then more than three decades later, I got an opportunity to get reacquainted with my country, perhaps for the first time in my capacity as an adult. I spent five years there. It stole my heart, and now that I have returned home to the United States, I feel a longing in my heart for my country and my people. But the moment I step on Indian soil, it starts to drive me crazy. Nothing functions smoothly, going to a bank is a full-day ordeal, no one believes in lines or waiting for their turn—I could go on and on. And yet the fruit vendor, the cabbie, the rickshaw guys will go to the ends of the earth to help you in whatever way they can. They have so little, but they have generosity of spirit in abundance. I guess such is my country with its multiple personality disorder.

After coming back from India, I have been feeling very heavy with the weight of grief and loss. My final act for Ma was to empty her house and dispose of all her earthly belongings. I tried to do the best I could, but I do not know whether I did what Ma would have wanted. This act gave me pause. I do not have children; I am not sure how my stuff will get purged. So I have started purging now.

Relationships are never stagnant. They are always evolving. Either they are getting stronger or moving apart. Sometimes relationships start to move apart. It's nobody's fault—they just do. We often try to cling to the glory of what they were, how it was, and how it ought to be. Because it was great, how can it not be so anymore? I think the thing to do is to let go gracefully and preserve the wonderful memories. If not, those incredible memories will be replaced by the struggles of trying to go against the flow in trying to hang on. Perhaps if it is meant to be, a stronger relationship will emerge in time, but one thing is for certain: it cannot and will not be the same.

Before I moved to India to take care of Ma, I had many deep social relationships and was involved with many things. My absence from my universe as I knew it led to a vanishing of me from it. I came back and struggled to find my place in my own universe. The void I had left quickly filled with other things and other people. This is the nature of absences and voids. It is akin to scooping a glass full of water from a bucket of water and then expecting the void created by the missing water to remain. It does not, and it cannot. Voids fill up. It actually is very scientific.

My previous thought led me to the following insight. When one creates something, one becomes the center of it. Let us call the creator "Creator" and the creation "Creation 1." Creation 1 grows up and acquires a life of its own. After acquiring a life of its own, Creation 1 forces Creator from the center to the fringes. Observation reveals that Creation 1 then creates something and becomes the center of the new creation, "Creation 2." Creation 2 then acquires a life of its own, and Creation 1 finds itself unexpectedly marginalized. Meanwhile, Creator, after a suitable period of moping and recovering, re-creates and becomes the center of this new creation, Creation 3, remaining its center until Creation 3 also grows up and pushes Creator out. Each of the creations creates, remains the center for a while, gets pushed out by the very creation it created, and then if it is lucky, is able to re-create. And the cycle repeats itself. Creation, center, fringe, hurt, re-creation, center, fringe, hurt, and so on and so forth. I have personally experienced this in family life. Parents give birth, and they are the center of the universe for the infant. Child grows up and puts the same parents on the fringes of its circle, of which it is now the center. The child then procreates, and the resulting progeny marginalizes its parents, who find themselves accompanying their parents whom they had marginalized. This cycle repeats ad infinitum. In a professional setting too, the same cycle of being the center followed by marginalization occurs. When we founded our company, we were the center. The organization grew and put us, the founders, on the fringes. The center is forever shifting. This is the very nature of creation. I wonder if God feels the same way. Marginalized by the very creation he created. If anyone thinks they can maintain position and control for more than a few fleeting moments, they are in for a very rude surprise and a tremendous loss of power and energy; trying to remain at the

center when the center is using all its youthful energy to push one
to the fringes is not trivial. I now understand what they mean by
"go with the flow"—the path of least resistance. It is best to let go
gracefully when one feels the push. Else pushed out one will be,
but with disgrace. Ma understood this innately and had learned to
let go. This is where her grace and elegance came from.

I took care of Ma for five years. It was a pretty tough time. I felt good about doing the right thing. After the tenure ended, I was convinced that life would do right by me. Not sure what I was expecting life to do for me, but I found myself struggling like I have not struggled before. Did not see that coming. COVID-19 and the political situation in the US made things even worse. But then I thought about it. To do away with an expectation and notion of fairness and justice is very liberating. When you expect good to happen because you did the right thing, and it does not, the mind immediately thinks, I must not have done good enough, otherwise how could this happen? But if the notion of justice is dispensed with, whether for good or for bad, what is left is just how it is. I think it may be easier to accept the missing reward than to see a wrongdoer not get his just deserts. But this is life. It just happens.

Dear Life,

You must have noticed that after concluding my mission in India and returning to the United States, I decided to stop coloring my hair. As the salt and pepper turned saltier, I realized I needn't have been envious of Harry Potter's invisibility cloak. All I needed was to have patience. Slowly but surely, life and age started to gently shroud me with one. I did not see it coming, nor did I feel it being put on me, but one day I found that the cloak was starting to work. Invisibility was starting to set in. A few more years and my cloak will work to perfection. I now see how we as a society make our elders invisible. I remembered Ma. She too had become invisible, but she had mastered the art of letting go gracefully and accepting life as it unfolded. I have a lot to learn.

Yours truly,
The Ordinary Human

My uncle passed away today. He was my mother's half-brother. They had the same father. Ma was very fond of him. She was sixteen when he was born and took care of him as her own baby. This uncle was an exceedingly difficult person to be around. He was very miserable in all his life choices, and he shared his misery generously every time he came to our place. The stories did not change. I would be full of unhappy anticipation every time a visit from him was scheduled. I had not called him in a while. And today I am filled with regret. The grief and sadness I am feeling at his passing have taken me by surprise. I never knew how much he really meant to me until now. I have heard this before, that people do not realize how much someone means to them until they lose them. Until today, mostly I have known how much people have meant to me, and when faced with their loss, there has been no element of surprise, only grief. My uncle will always be special for teaching me not to take people and relationships for granted. I miss you, my dear uncle, and I love you. I did not know that until today. I hope you are at peace. I do not know about reincarnation, but if it is there, I hope you have a happy and fulfilling next life. You loved your mother, and you even built a shrine in her memory. You and I have that love for a mother in common. When I moved to India to take care of my mother, you were the one person who really understood and acknowledged that and blessed me from your heart. Blessings I shall always cherish. Be at peace, my dear uncle.

In my unique journey, I experienced my share of grief and loss. I am not alone in having experienced this. A dear friend lost his son, a young man in the prime of his youth. An accident. I had no idea what to say. All we have is language to express ourselves. When expressing grief in the form of condolences, language fails us. There is nothing we can say to the one who has lost a loved one that will either lessen their grief or provide some relief. Words are insufficient, and language fails us. Yet we must condole because it is necessary for us to express empathy. It is necessary for the person bearing the loss to feel that people share in their grief and that they have support during this terrible tragedy. And society dictates it. Despite the failure of language, it is a necessary process. So I hugged my friend and told him how sorry I was for his loss. I clearly felt incomplete, because this expression was nowhere close to what needed to be communicated. My friend said thanks, and I could tell he was incomplete because how could the expression of apology compensate for the magnitude of the loss? Yet we understood each other and just hugged.

The subtitle of this book refers to "random ramblings." After I returned from India, while trying to figure out reentry, I had plenty of time for thoughts that were even more random in nature than most of the random ones in this collection thus far. I share one of my favorite ones with you. I love language. In addition to giving us the ability to communicate, it also gives us a mechanism to hide. We have learned to use language to say the opposite of what we actually mean. We have also learned to preface our sentences with disclaimers so as to move away from responsibility. Here are a few of my favorite examples. "To be honest . . ." What an incredible lead in. Leads one to believe that the speaker is a person of great integrity. But upon closer analysis, it makes one wonder why some sentences would need to be prefaced thusly. Shouldn't all communication have a presumption of honesty, making this preface redundant? Then there is the preface, "I don't mean to, but . . ." I absolutely love this one. The moment we start a sentence with "I do not mean to" followed by a "but," we absolutely mean to say and do exactly what we declare our intention to not be. Another one of my favorites is "If truth were to be told." Why would truth not be told? Isn't it an undesirable situation if it would change the status quo if truth were in fact to be told? Another gem we use to avoid responsibility starts with "I was unable to" or "I couldn't." We do not like saying, "I didn't." I think "couldn't" or "unable to" indicates circumstances outside our control, whereas "I didn't" places responsibility on us. And the incredible thing is, we all, without exception, self included, use language in this way and find it acceptable when others do the same. I find this fascinating.

A nother truly random rambling alert. I am of the opinion that social media is anything but social. I think Facebook in particular (I say Facebook, for I do not know Instagram and other social media platforms as well) is a display of "look how good my life is," perhaps in an attempt to convince oneself more than others. There is a brilliant Toyota Venza car commercial[9] that illustrates this point beautifully. In the commercial, a young woman is sitting alone in her home with her computer and talking, and the commercial cuts in and out of high-activity and high-energy images of her parents driving a Toyota Venza, meeting up with their friends, riding bicycles, and having a wonderful time. Meanwhile, this is what the daughter is saying: "I read [. . .] an online article about how older people are becoming more and more antisocial. So I was really aggressive with my parents about joining Facebook. My parents are up to nineteen friends now. I have six hundred and eighty-seven friends. This is living." She is sitting alone with her list of 687 friends while her parents are having fun with presumably two of the nineteen they have. Whoever authored this commercial is a kindred spirit.

I see these types of messages on social media often: "Lord, please protect all my family." And I hear the lord say, "Define family." I wonder about this statement because, in this prayer, who are we asking the lord to protect? Is it our parents and siblings? Does it include our aunts and uncles and first cousins? What about second cousins? What about our parents' first and second cousins? What about those whom we love more than family, like best friends and other relationships that one cannot pin down? If we are asking an all-merciful lord to protect our family, the lord does not know who to protect and who to leave out. Why do we limit our request to just our family even if we are able to define that word? Is it because we think that the omnipotent lord's resources and capabilities are limited, or is it because we are selfish, and we want to be better protected than our neighbor? To follow this thought to its logical conclusion, I am not protected unless all of humanity is protected. What better evidence of it than in these very trying times of COVID? Our prayer must be to protect all of humanity.

Ma has been gone for two years now. It is not that Ma's memory is fading. But I am finally starting to feel like myself again. The pain, loss, and grief are still there, but the guilt, the anguish, the fatigue, and the anger are taking a back seat. I can think of Ma with much less pain and remember her more with love and fondness.

I remember once, a while back, when Ma was independent and healthy, I used to talk to her every morning on my drive to work. That half hour was our mother-daughter time. Mostly, it was me complaining about work or people or about whatever happened to be the *woe du jure*. Mostly Ma would lend a sympathetic ear. One day, she said something to me that altered my relationship to challenges and struggles. After listening to me go on for a while, she said, "The story is in the struggle." She elaborated that the moment a story hits "and they lived happily ever after," there is no more left to be said. Not one word. I was stunned into silence by the power of this insight. This insight has stayed with me since, and every time I feel bogged down by life, I remember her words and think, "This is my story unfolding."

Ramesh Harjani

Dear Mani,[10]

You are my evidence that I must have done something right; you could not have been given to just anyone.

I am filled with gratitude every time I count my blessings. And the biggest one in that long list is you—my friend, my husband, and my life companion. You bring love, fun, joy, laughter, and adventure to my life. I do not say this in a clichéd way, but I give you evidence:

You are someone who wears and makes me wear a Peaky Blinders cap anytime we watch anything British, which is often.

You are someone who tenderly extended an arm from behind with a white linen shirt sleeve rolled down so I could wipe my snot and tears when caught off guard by emotions at a wedding.

You are someone who scribbles on a piece of toilet paper and turns that idea into a patent.

You are someone who drives seven hours one way to Chicago to pick up takeaway so as to satisfy a food craving.

You are someone who lets his nieces paint his toes and then displays them proudly.

You are the gentlest person I know who is as tough as nails.

I asked of you the unreasonable, and you generously gave me the impossible. You kept your word about seeing Ma through.

You are my linchpin of happiness, luck, success, and just my all-around good luck talisman. Without you, my everything will unravel. I asked to grow old with you. And here we are forty years later. You are my silver fox and I now your zebra. I hope that we have reached no more than the halfway point of our togetherness. My ultimate wish for us: may we be so lucky as to exit this planet together.

Thank you for a journey most magnificent, my dearest friend!

With love and gratitude,
Savi

Acknowledgments

I am in awe of the Universe and all the people in it that have inspired these musings. I am inadequately equipped to thank everyone by name who has contributed to making this book possible, for that in itself would be a book of infinite pages.

My head first bows in gratitude and humility to my parents, Kanta and Sagar Chand Gupta. I am not sure what I did to deserve this privilege of being born their daughter. The only explanation I can come up with is either some karmic credit from another lifetime or the happiest, most random happenstance of my life. I had an incredibly happy and secure childhood. I wanted for nothing and was showered with love. I was given the freedom to fail and yet be unconditionally loved. I was taught to think outside the lines of conformity. Both my parents have passed on, yet they continue to parent me every single day. I draw upon the lessons taught expressly and the wisdom and guidance imparted silently by example. Their words and teachings echo in my mind and guide me every single day, and the memory of their smiles and gentle touch comforts me in my difficult times.

I come from a small family unit, mom, dad, brother, and self. Etched in my mind is an image of an old black-and-white photograph of a seven-year-old boy holding a two-day-old baby sister and lifting her up to his face to try and kiss her—my older brother, Arvind Gupta. As a child, I grew up under the protection of my big brother. Anytime I ran into a problem, my brother was there. He sheltered me from the outside world and advocated for me on the inside to my parents. As grown-ups, we have lived continents apart, but that bond of unwavering love is exactly that—unwavering. I have always looked up to my big brother, and I always will. I thank him for always encouraging me to write and share my thoughts with the world. I thank Arvind for writing the introduction to this book and for being a bit more generous with his words than was warranted.

I acknowledge my younger brother, Om Prakash Thakur, Omi. I think Ma liked him best and he took amazing care of her. Omi epitomizes love, loyalty, commitment, and strength. He is my brother and I and my family owe him a great debt of gratitude.

Yet again, the Universe comes to my aid in getting this book published in the form of a force of nature called Aila Malik. Aila is my niece-in-law, and with her as your coach, mentor, and champion, it is impossible to verbalize a goal and then not have it be realized. Aila is herself a published author and has played the role of my book doctor. She is the one who informed me that there was a "there, there" for my musings. Thank you, Aila!

I believe that people step into what is expected of them. And here, I must express my undying gratitude to all my family, friends, colleagues, and teachers for expecting me to succeed when I did not think it possible. This book would not have been possible without your love, support, and encouragement.

My thanks to the elders in my family, who taught me right from wrong. In particular, my thanks to my aunt Vidya Verma and my parents-in-law, Gul and Gulab Harjani. My gratitude to the Mittal family—Drs. Ashok Mittal, Santosh Mittal, Aneesh Mittal, and Sanjeev Mitla. Ashok Bhaisahab[11] has always been there for me and my family, such has been his regard for my parents. And such was my parents' trust in him that my father called him his "one-man army," and my ma made him the executor of her will. Immense gratitude for Santosh Bhaisahab; he was instrumental in helping Ma get the best medical care possible. I am grateful to Sanjeev for helping me give closure to Ma's earthly possessions. And I thank Aneesh for introducing me to the artist for this book.

I have the unique privilege of being the youngest in my generation on my maternal and paternal sides, even among my in-laws of my generation. This status has given me special privileges with all my brothers and sisters. They have loved me and protected me. And reluctantly, I will admit, even spoiled me a little. My thanks to my brothers and sisters by virtue of marriage, either mine or my brother's—Jayanti Gupta, Kiran and Sunny Harjani, Neelam and Naresh Harjani, Chand and Anup Bhargava, and Angella and Rajiv Rimal. I am particularly indebted to my sister-in-law Dr. Chand Bhargava. Her love, support, and medical guidance was critical in the care of Ma. My thanks to my maternal cousins and their significant others—we were never cousins, always siblings. Anisha and Kailash Malhotra, Vijaya and Deepak Verma, Anita and Jyoti Tamuli, Sunil Varma, Sunita Menon, Geeta Varma, Meenakshi Rajput, and Navin Virmani. In particular, I thank Anita for always being there whenever Ma and I needed her help. I thank my paternal cousins and their families for their love—SP Mittal, Sadhna and Anil Mittal, Sandhya and Naresh Tanwar, Shalini and Anuj Mittal, Rachna and Anil Sahni, and Sarita and Naresh Gupta. I am very grateful to Anil for holding my hand and being by my side at the cremation ground as we performed the last rites for Ma.

I never had children of my own. My love and thanks to all my nieces, nephews, grandnieces, and grandnephews who have fulfilled me as a mother. I thank Anisha Karn and Johnny Harjani, Shalini Poddar and Tony Harjani, Pavan Harjani, Priyansha Silwal and Kushal Harjani, Varsha Bhargava and Upamanyu Mukhopadhyay, Aastha Dua and Saagar Bhargava, Anisha Singh and Harsh Nayyar, Prachi Singh, Sabina Diaz-Rimal, Vivek Gupta, Abhishek Gupta, Tina Doshi and Akshay Verma, Aila Malik and Kapil Verma, Aseem Malhotra, Jyotsna Kashyap and Roderick Mitchell, Nayana Jha and Michael Cain, Yamini Jha-Korman and Daniel Korman, Zayan Verma, Kenza Verma, Kaysan Verma, Dylan Verma, Jordan Verma, Nikhil Korman, Bodhi Mitchell, and Neel Mukhopadhyay. I am enormously grateful to Pavan, who stood by my side and helped me take care of Ma in her last days. A giant thanks to Prachi, who despite being the youngest has been my sounding board these many years.

I am lucky that I love the family I was given. But I am even luckier in my choice of friends who have become family. I thank you all for your love and friendship. Sipra (an important pillar of my life—we have shared so much) and Prabhakara Jha, Pikka Sodhi and Manindra Singh, Karen and Anurag Narula, Suranjoy Hazarika, Debu Purohit, Ofelia Ferran and Sachin Sapatnekar, Janice Noruk and Rama Murthy, Ibha Kumari, Serena and John Wright, Sidney Sasser, and Neeti and Deepak Dave. My gratitude for these dynamic young people whose friendship I cherish— Ami Dave, Sara Lederman, Monika Mittal, Neha Puri, Anjali Narula, and Rakesh Ankit. I am grateful for the camaraderie of colleagues who have become lifelong friends—Tammie Follett, Carol Stenback, and Jim Bush. Tammie is plugged into an infinite source of energy and has been inspiring me since the first day we met. Thank you, Tammie, for being my mentor, champion, and friend. Michael Olenick, Lisa Hansen, and Kirsten Rodger Storlie—my dear friends from law school, thank you for being the company that misery loved. My gratitude for Leija and Scott DeLisi, dear friends who encouraged me to share my writing. My heartfelt thanks to SP Dubey and Mukesh Gupta, who are an integral part of my family and whose contribution toward the care of my mother was nothing less than awe-inspiring. Without each and every one of you, life would have been very dull and not worth musing about.

To my dearest childhood friends, our bonds are foundational and will last a lifetime. We got into enough mischief then, and I hope we will continue to do so until the very end. Thank you Shipra Tyagi, Puneet Talwar, Ritu Ahuja, Malini Mathur, Molly Som, Ramakant Mehra, Bipin Bharadwaj, Subhasis Ojha, Piyush Gupta, Nikunj Goel, Neeraj Agarwal, Naresh Yadav, Parth Sharma, Anila Prabhu, Chandana Asthana, Nibedita Sharma, and Vivek Mathur. My undying gratitude to Piyush for defying the wrath of COVID and coming to stand by me as I bid my mother a final goodbye. I am so grateful for Naresh Yadav's friendship and help in the care of my mother.

I thank all my teachers for teaching me and believing in me. Without you, I would not be equipped to communicate even one single thought, let alone so many random ones. Specifically, my thanks to Mrs. Usha Bhalla, who believed in me and adopted me as one of her own. I am reminded of one particular teacher who may be disappointed in me though. I must have been an annoying kid in class because as we were graduating high school, she wrote in my farewell diary, "Curiosity with knowledge is better than idle curiosity." I am sorry to report, ma'am, that even four decades later, I have not been able to mend my ways. This book, *Postcards from Within,* is still largely a work comprised of idle curiosity and random observations of humans and humanity.

And finally, my immense gratitude to all those who taught me the toughest lessons of my life. Without you, I would not have grown as a human being—thank you!

ACKNOWLEDGMENTS FOR MY PROFESSIONAL TEAM

I am enormously grateful to my professional team for making my debut journey as an author possible and exciting.

Illustrator and Artist

Arushi Mittal is a freelance artist studying fashion design at the School of the Art Institute of Chicago. She designed my book cover and the illustrations. Arushi peeked inside my head and captured the images precisely as I had envisioned them. She has done a brilliant job. This journey would have been incomplete without her. Thank you, Arushi!

Beaver's Pond Press

I am very grateful to the Beaver's Pond team for bringing my project from an audience of one to the world. My particular thanks to Lily Coyle, Laurie Herrmann, Caitlin Fultz, Rachel Blood, and Evan Allgood for educating me and gently guiding me to make the right decisions. Thank you all!

James Monroe Design

James Monroe designed my book and my website and did a phenomenal job. His designs have given life in perpetuity to my book. Thank you, Jay!

Endnotes

1. *Pukka dost* means best friend. Ma used to call me her "pukka dosht," pronouncing the "dost" affectionately as "dosht."
2. *Bhai* is a Hindi word meaning "brother."
3. "Shrödinger's Cat." Wikipedia, last modified December 27, 2022, https://en.wikipedia.org/wiki/Schr%C3%B6dinger%27s_cat.
4. K. Baclawski, "The Observer Effect," abstract, *2018 IEEE Conference on Cognitive and Computational Aspects of Situation Management (CogSIMA)*, https://www.doi.org/10.1109/COGSIMA.2018.8423983.
5. Born on October 2, "Mahatma Gandhi was the leader of India's non-violent independence movement against British rule." "Mahatma Gandhi." Biography.com, last modified September 4, 2019, https://www.biography.com/activist/mahatma-gandhi.
6. "Great Trial of 1922." Mahatma Gandhi's Writings, Philosophy, Audio, Video, and Photographs, https://www.mkgandhi.org/speeches/gto1922.htm.
7. *Didi* means "older sister" in Hindi.
8. I am using the male pronoun for God because I am using the male pronoun for God. It is not a statement on issues relating to gender equality.
9. Toyota Venza commercial, https://www.youtube.com/watch?v=1xEMNrSdkdY.
10. Mani is what I call my husband, Ramesh.
11. *Bhaisahab* is a term of respect for an older brother.

ABOUT THE AUTHOR

Savita Harjani was born in Bombay and grew up in New Delhi, India. She moved to the United States when she was twenty years old. She has lived in Pittsburgh, Pennsylvania, and Santa Clara, California, and for the past thirty-two years has been living in Minneapolis, Minnesota. She studied law at Hamline University School of Law. Savita started her legal career working at Thomson Reuters and later transitioned to legal consulting, wherein she created a niche strategic-legal-management model. In 2016, Savita paused her professional life and moved to India to take care of her mother. After completing her tenure as a caregiver in 2020, Savita decided to not return to the profession and retired from the active practice of law. She is now exploring her second career as a writer in the third act of her life, starting with her debut work, *Postcards from Within,* a memoir.